WEALTH BUILDING
101

Other Books in the Trump University Series

Trump University Real Estate 101: Building Wealth with Real Estate Investments

Trump University Marketing 101: How to Use the Most Powerful Ideas in Marketing to Get More Customers to Keep Them

Trump University Entrepreneurship 101: How to Turn Your Ideas into a Money Machine

Trump University Asset Protection 101: Tax and Legal Strategies of the Rich

TRUMP
UNIVERSITY

WEALTH BUILDING
101

Your First
90 Days on the
Path to Prosperity

EDITED BY DONALD J. TRUMP
PREFACE AND CHAPTER 1 BY DONALD J. TRUMP

JOHN WILEY & SONS, INC.

Published by John Wiley & Sons, Inc., Hoboken, New Jersey.
Published simultaneously in Canada.
Wiley Bicentennial Logo: Richard J. Pacifico

For general information on our other products and services or for technical support, please
contact our Customer Care Department within the United States at (800) 762-2974, outside
the United States at (317) 572-3993 or fax (317) 572-4002.

Wiley also publishes its books in a variety of electronic formats. Some content that appears in
print may not be available in electronic books. For more information about Wiley products,
visit our web site at www.wiley.com.

Library of Congress Cataloging-in-Publication Data:
  Trump University wealth building 101 : your first 90 days on the path to prosperity / edited
by Donald J. Trump; managing editor Dorianne R. Perrucci.
    p. cm.
  "Published simultaneously in Canada."
  ISBN 978-0-470-10016-5 (cloth : alk paper)
1. Success in business. 2. Entrepreneurship. 3. Wealth. 4. Investments. 5. Finance,
Personal. I. Trump, Donald, 1946– II. Perrucci, Dorianne R., 1949– III. Trump
University. IV. Title: Wealth building 101.
  HF5386.T81496 2007
  332.024'01—dc22

                                                                          2007016882

ISBN-13: 978-0-470-10016-5

Printed in the United States of America

10 9 8 7 6 5 4 3 2 1

CONTENTS

CONTENTS

CONTENTS

FOREWORD

If you dedicate yourself to applying the strategies in *Trump University Wealth Building 101*, you will become wealthy. If you make this book part of your life, it will make you rich.

I can make those statements with complete confidence because *Trump University Wealth Building 101* is built on the same foundation as all Trump University publications and courses. We deliver practical, proven instruction from people who have actually done what they are teaching you. Other organizations try to sell hope alone, without the proven expertise to back it up, and just when you begin to realize that the advice you paid for is unproven and ineffective—they try to sell you more expensive products. They hook you on promises and never deliver.

Neither I nor our chairman, Donald J. Trump, would stand for that at Trump University. We are building Trump University on "how to" information in the purest sense. After all, what could be more powerful than proven advice that you can follow step by step?

This philosophy of learning comes from Donald J. Trump, who holds Trump University accountable for creating an institution that teaches people to become successful from the moment their studies begin, not at some hazy point in the future. In these pages, our team of experts sets out practical, proven, step-by-step advice that helps you achieve significant success.

How Will This Book Make You Wealthy?

That's a fair question, so let me give you a road map.

Part I (Chapters 1–3)—You learn to unleash your "inner Trump" from Mr. Trump himself, as he explains how *he* thinks about wealth in Chapter 1. In Chapters 2 and 3, you develop your "wealth mindset" and learn the habits that bring success.

Part II (Chapters 4–6)—You make plans that will turn your dreams of wealth into reality. You learn to create a vision of your financial future—then assemble the tools, people, and resources to make it come true.

Part III (Chapters 7–9)—Get your financial house in order. You learn to master seven critical practices that set very wealthy people apart from everyone else. Eliminate debt and develop wealth-maximizing routines.

Parts IV, V, and VI offer you three alternative paths to creating wealth. You can apply one of them, or two, or all three, depending on your interests, strengths, and ambitions.

Part IV (Chapters 10–12)—You master the secrets of starting or buying a business and running it successfully because owning your own business is one of the best ways to get rich.

Part V (Chapters 13–15)—Real estate remains the foundation of wealth. Step-by-step instructions from the Trump University faculty show you how to get started, then expand your holdings to create both cash income and long-term appreciation. Real estate is where sizeable wealth is expanded and maintained.

Part VI (Chapters 16–17)—Master the basics of investing in stocks and bonds—then learn how to create a balanced, diversified portfolio of investments the way that top investors do. Secure your future with techniques for growing your retirement nest egg.

Part VII (Chapters 18–20)—In this final step, you discover Trump-powered techniques for keeping your hard-earned money—and growing it—for the rest of your life. Minimize your taxes, profit now from estate planning, and protect your assets from the tax collector.

Make Trump University Part of Your Wealth-Building Plan

Before you turn to page 1 and start on the road to substantial riches, let me share one more important insight with you: Achieving significant wealth requires a constant flow of new information.

Growing very rich is not a static activity. It requires you to keep learning and applying new knowledge and new techniques. In the years to come, for example, new laws will be enacted that will affect your investments. In the real estate universe, new mortgages will appear that offer powerful new ways to finance your property purchases—or pose considerable risks to the unwary.

There are always new strategies to learn and apply. As we go to press with this book, it is a great time to invest in real estate foreclosures. That is why Trump University developed a new course, *The Real Estate Foreclosure Coaching Program*, to address that need. But the boom in foreclosures might end in six months. And when that happens, there will be other strategies to learn and apply.

Wealth building is, and always will be, a lot like hitting a moving target from a galloping horse. That's why Trump University is here for you. Our flexibility and speed allow us, more quickly than traditional institutions of higher learning, to anticipate money-creating trends and offer instruction on the spot.

So put the advice in this book to work and build your wealth. But get involved with Trump University, too, so your knowledge and skills stay fresh.

If you apply that one-two combination for becoming rich, you simply cannot lose.

MICHAEL SEXTON

PRESIDENT, TRUMP UNIVERSITY
NEW YORK CITY

PREFACE

Early in my career, it became obvious to me that education gives you a big edge in business. When you learn everything you can about what you're getting into, risk—which is always a part of doing business—is substantially reduced. People who are more educated—by that I mean savvy and prepared, not just formally educated—have the advantage. That's what has made me so successful.

Trump University, the unique online learning experience I established in May of 2005, grew out of my desire to share my business knowledge. There's a huge demand for practical, convenient education that teaches success. I'm an active presence in shaping the curricula, and publishing books like *Wealth Building 101*, because I truly believe in the power of education and its function as an engine of success. Unlike the exclusive apartments and offices I build, Trump University is *inclusive*. It's all about leveling the playing field. Not everyone who wants to get ahead can drop everything and go to business school as I did. Not everyone has the time or the money. Not everyone has the connections.

I want Trump University and *Wealth Building 101* to help you write your own success story. That's why I invited the contributors to work on this book with me. They're a great team. Some of them teach at Trump University, but all of them have real-world knowledge and run successful businesses. They can teach you how to build wealth for yourself.

Here's a tip for getting the most out of this book. Don't get overwhelmed by all the good ideas and the details. The book is organized into seven simple steps. Focus on how you can implement these steps in the next 90 days. If you do, I guarantee it will put you on the path to prosperity, just like the subtitle says. Most people never take the time to come up with even a basic plan for building wealth and becoming financially secure—so by learning from the experts in this book, you are way ahead of the game. So read about it, but more importantly go do it!

DONALD J. TRUMP

About the Authors

John R. Burley has been actively investing for over a quarter of a century and has completed over 1,000 real estate deals. John spent several years as a top financial planner and has valuable insider information to share about the industry in the first six chapters. At the age of 32, rather than retire, he chose to continue to invest while teaching others how to become financially free. He is the author of *Money Secrets of the Rich* and *Powerful Changes*, and teaches a Real Estate Investing Boot Camp. For more information, visit www.johnburley.com.

J. J. Childers is a licensed attorney specializing in "wealth structures" that reduce taxes and shield assets. He speaks on these topics to thousands of individuals, investors, and small business owners each year. He is also an active investor and small business owner himself. His unique ability to explain complicated strategies in simple terms has made him one of the nation's most sought after speakers and practitioners on asset-protecting legal structures. For more information, see www.secretmillionaire.com.

Gary W. Eldred, PhD, the best-selling author of *The Beginner's Guide to Real Estate Investing* (Hoboken, NJ: John Wiley & Sons, 2004) and many other books on real estate, serves as Trump University's chief content expert for its Real Estate Investor Training Program. Gary is a veteran real estate buyer, seller, and investment consultant. He has taught graduate courses on real estate at some of America's top universities, including Stanford University, the University of Illinois, and the University of Virginia. For more information, visit www.garyeldred.com.

Michael E. Gordon, PhD, is the author of *Trump University Entrepreneurship 101: How to Turn Your Idea into a Money Machine* (Hoboken, NJ: John Wiley & Sons, 2007). Michael teaches corporate entrepreneurship at universities around the world and to date has started six successful companies. Currently, he is president of www.AngelDeals.com, an Internet business that helps entrepreneurs find funding, and the Center for Competitive Success (www.CompetitiveSuccess.com), a management consultancy. He is an adjunct professor at Babson College, the Harvard University Extension School, and the International School of Management in Paris.

Richard Parker is recognized as the leading authority on buying small businesses. He is an author and business acquisition consultant who has bought 10 businesses and started several more, written eight books, and is the resident expert for BizQuest.com. One of the country's most successful small business intermediaries, Richard, who founded the Diomo Corporation (diomo.com), has helped small business buyers in over 70 countries. He is also the author of *The Art of Buying a Business* published by Trump University. This comprehensive guide is the real deal—not a theoretical classroom discussion—from an entrepreneur who's "been there, done that." To learn more, visit www.TrumpUniversity.com/wealthbuilding101.

Philip A. Springer, president of Retirement Wealth Management, Inc., is a leading authority on building and enjoying a rich retirement. From 1995 to 2001, Philip was editor of *The Retirement Letter,* a leading national source of independent information and advice. A popular speaker at investment conferences and on investment cruises, Philip has been interviewed on CNBC, CNN, and written articles for or been quoted in many national publications, including *BusinessWeek, Kiplinger's Personal Finance,* the *New York Times,* and the *Wall Street Journal.* For more information, see his web site, www.wealthretirement.com.

Marshall Sylver, is considered the leading authority on subconscious reprogramming and subconscious influence. He lectures before over 250,000 people live every year. He has appeared on David Letterman, Donny Doutche, Montel Williams, and many more. Over $150,000,000 of his books and training programs have been sold in many languages worldwide over the last decade. His speaking skills have earned him well over $1,000,000 in just one day. He is known in the industry as a "Trainers Trainer" for his ability to powerfully sell and influence from the stage. Top speakers and trainers worldwide pay Marshall up to $30,000 per hour to consult with him. He is also known as "The Greatest Hypnotist of All Time" and hosts the world's largest hypnotic production show on the main stage of Harrah's Hotel and Casino in Las Vegas. His live daily radio show can be heard on the web at www.sylver.com. A true renaissance man, he is an entertainer, educator, and author.

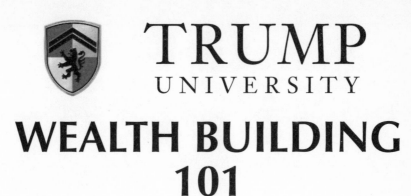

WEALTH BUILDING
101

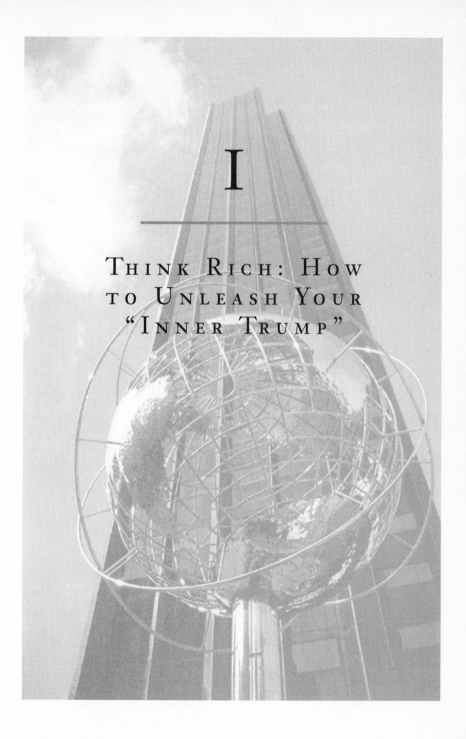

I

THINK RICH: HOW TO UNLEASH YOUR "INNER TRUMP"

1

BUILD WEALTH—MY WAY

by

Donald J. Trump

Through trial and error I've learned how to do a lot of things the right way over the years, and I want to share this knowledge with you. To be successful, you've got to learn and develop these 12 skills:

1. Get passionate.
2. Be tenacious.
3. Think big.
4. Leverage knowledge.
5. Be thorough.
6. Take action.
7. Take risks.
8. Know your audience.
9. Learn to negotiate.
10. Listen to your gut.
11. Enjoy competition.
12. Be your own best asset.

Let's take it one step at a time.

GET PASSIONATE

Passion sounds out of place in business, but it's at the top of my list. I know for a fact—and from my own experience—that it's absolutely critical to achieving any kind of long-lasting success.

Exactly what is passion?

Enthusiasm on a big scale. If you don't have passion, everything you do will fizzle, or at best, be mediocre. You simply have to love what you do to make it big. People with passion never give up because they never have a reason to give up, regardless of their circumstances. It's an intangible momentum that can make you indomitable.

How do you get passion?

Size up your interests. What do you love doing? Ask yourself, "Can I develop any of these interests into a viable source of income? Can I come up with a personal blueprint? Do I have a foundation in place, or in the works, for this blueprint?"

Cover your bases—and then act. Very often the dividing line between success and failure is a lack of passion. I've known people who have had fantastic ideas, but they don't get them off the ground, and their ideas sit in their head or on top of their desk for a long time. Coming up with an idea is not enough—you've got to put your idea into action.

BE TENACIOUS

People think I was born with the Midas touch, and I admit, I've been very fortunate. I got a great education from the schools I attended, and from my parents. But I learned to be tenacious when I started in business. That's important, because most things don't happen overnight.

As I write this chapter, we're on schedule to finish Trump Place along the Hudson River in New York City by 2008. With 16 buildings, it's the largest development ever approved by the New York City Planning Commission and will transform the once-neglected West Side of Manhattan into a very desirable place for residents to live. I bought the land in 1974. That's a long time to wait. If I hadn't been tenacious, Trump Place would still be in my head.

Tenacity is when you refuse to give in or give up. You keep fighting the good fight. Very few things of worth are easy achievements. That's just the way it works.

Tenacity enables you to work through obstacles and problems along the way without becoming worn down or negative. In fact, you should expect problems, so you don't waste energy.

Tenacity is when you keep moving forward. You don't allow fear to paralyze you.

Sometimes the most talented people fail, while those far less talented succeed. Why? Because those who succeed move forward with confidence.

I don't accept excuses in this area, so get to work!

THINK BIG

When you were a child, would you have liked to keep crawling, when everyone else was walking? I don't think so.

We all have to start with small steps, but the point is: Get to the biggest steps you're capable of taking. Thinking small will limit your potential. Thinking big will take you places. Thinking big can get you to the top, and I can tell you, it's not lonely up here.

Successful people like challenges. It's our nature. Keep in sync with this basic premise, and you'll begin moving forward with the momentum necessary for great achievement.

Striving from an early age is one secret to success. I learned to work hard from an early age, trying to catch up with my father who was a very successful developer. But you can keep striving no matter what your age or accomplishments.

These three tips will guide you:

1. Ask yourself why your plans are so small. Then begin to expand your horizons.
2. Concentrate on managing your future, not your past. Learn from the past, but don't stay there.
3. Look at the solution. Don't focus on the problem.

LEVERAGE KNOWLEDGE

When I was waiting for the opportunity to buy 40 Wall Street, which became the home of Trump University, I spent time studying the building and the area, and kept informed. When the opportunity finally came, I was ready and I knew what I was getting into. I knew the building, and I knew why the owners were having trouble managing it. As a result, I was able to buy this 1.3 million-square-foot landmark, the tallest building in lower Manhattan, for a mere $1 million in 1995.

So when I say knowledge is power, I mean it. Use it to your advantage.

But knowledge is only the foundation of great enterprises. Einstein said that imagination is more important than knowledge. What he meant is: Without imagination and the ability to visualize possibilities, what would be the point of great knowledge?

An example is how I develop golf courses. I get the best experts in the world, and I ask them hundreds of questions. I go over every detail, every tree, every hole, and every idea with them. Fortunately, they love what they do, so they don't find my questions tedious. By the time construction is underway, I know everything that's being done, and I can keep an informed eye on the progress.

Put imagination and knowledge together, and in no time you'll have something plenty big in your "think big tank."

Be Thorough

There's really no such thing as knowing too much about what you're doing.

When I was in college, I spent my spare time reading about real estate and foreclosures. I didn't feel it was a sacrifice of my time, because I was interested in real estate; I wasn't studying just to pass a test. The knowledge I gained on my own led to my first successful investment. I couldn't have achieved that if I hadn't spent the time studying on my own.

In college, I also read something that Rudyard Kipling wrote which I've never forgotten: "I keep six honest serving men, they taught me all I knew—their names are What and Why and When—and How and Where and Who." Finding the answers to these questions will ensure that your information is comprehensive and correct.

On *The Apprentice* when my associates and I interviewed candidates, sometimes the process went on for hours—one boardroom meeting lasted for over five hours so we could make the most knowledgeable decision possible.

Staying informed is a daily task and challenge, considering how quickly our world is moving. But not keeping up is like agreeing to check out—please don't do that. Plug in and learn everything you can. You never know when information will come in handy. If I hadn't studied real estate foreclosures as a student, I wouldn't have been able to see the great opportunity that led to my first big success.

Resolve to move forward and to learn as much as you can—today and every day.

TAKE ACTION

Knowledge alone isn't enough. You have to act on knowledge.

That's why we based one whole season of *The Apprentice* on this dichotomy, pitting a team of people with higher education who were "book smart," but clueless in the real world, against a team that was "street smart," but clueless about the right information.

Learning by doing challenges you to prove yourself.

My first big real estate job was turning around a 1,200-unit residential development with 800 vacant apartments that had become a disaster. The developers had gone under, and the government had foreclosed. I learned a lot, made a good profit, and got the confidence to take the next step in my real estate career. That wouldn't have happened if I hadn't put my knowledge to work for me. I studied and prepared, but then I took action.

Did you ever notice how easy some things look until you try them for yourself? Golf is like that. The sport looks effortless and even noncompetitive until you try to play. Suddenly, it takes on an entirely new dimension. The real pros make extremely difficult maneuvers look easy because they've spent hours perfecting their technique.

Don't underestimate anything until you've tried it for yourself.

Start practicing!

TAKE RISKS

Many people are afraid to fail, so they don't try. They talk, but they don't do. That's the perfect formula for failure.

My advice? Take some risks, even if you fail.

There has never been, and never will be, an Olympic ice skater who hasn't taken a spill on the ice, no matter how much he or she knew about ice skating. Skaters acquire their skills by doing, not by watching.

Take some risks, even if you get criticized and are afraid you don't know enough.

When I was interested in acquiring the (former) Commodore Hotel near Grand Central Station years ago, a friend told reporters my idea was like "fighting for a seat on the Titanic." Admittedly, I was working against great odds. The area around Grand Central had become really dilapidated, but the armchair critics made me wonder: Why not do something about it instead of just complaining?

Apply this thinking to yourself and to your situation. You'll not only learn a lot, but by taking risks you'll learn how much you didn't know, which is equally important. The new Hyatt Hotel next to Grand Central Terminal was a huge success for me, and sparked the redevelopment of the entire area.

Give yourself a challenge, not once in a while, but every day.

KNOW YOUR AUDIENCE

You've heard the phrase, "Life is a performance," and it's true. No matter what field you're in, large parts of life and business involve acting. Acting encompasses people skills, negotiation skills, public relations, salesmanship, and the ability to read your audience, whether your audience consists of four people in your office or 40,000 watching your television show.

Start by realizing that your audience can understand and appreciate many of your experiences. Make an effort to find out what you have in common, and lead with it. I may be a billionaire, but I have bad days just like everyone else. I get stuck in traffic jams, too.

If you take the time to think about what your audience wants, and what you have in common with them, you can create a bond that didn't exist before. It also frees you from being nervous and allows you to focus better. Think of yourself as a performer, with a responsibility to your audience (who may also be your customers). Showmanship means being prepared for every performance, and the more prepared you are, the more effective you will be. *Learn, know, and show:* It's a proven formula.

LEARN TO NEGOTIATE

Negotiation is one of the keys to business and life. Think of it as personal diplomacy. It can be complex, but it doesn't have to be daunting if you take the time to think and finesse your technique.

Learning to negotiate is invaluable if you hope to connect in any way with other people. You've got to understand where the other side is coming from if you want to succeed. Sometimes you can size that up quickly, sometimes not.

I remember negotiating with someone I didn't like very much, which put an invisible wall between us. Then I discovered that he was an avid golfer, like me. Suddenly we had something to talk about that we both enjoyed. Negotiations went much better after that. Comedians know how to play to their audience, so do the best public speakers. Learn from them.

Businesspeople see me as a master negotiator because I usually wind up with what I am aiming to get. I negotiate to win, and then I win. From the outside looking in, it looks simple, but I spend a lot of time preparing for any negotiation.

The first step is knowing exactly what you want. Be clear about your own goals. Then know what the other side wants. Now give that some thought. Whether you're in baseball or in business, you've got to know the strengths and weaknesses of your opponents to negotiate effectively. No two teams or companies are exactly the same.

Don't rely on generalizations. Find out for yourself.

For example, when I was hoping to acquire 40 Wall Street, I learned as much as I could about the Hinneberg family, who owned the building. Interested buyers, including me, were told to deal with the family's agent. But I wanted to know the Hinnebergs personally, to figure out what they wanted. If you want the truth, go to the source. So I flew to Germany and met with them. I told them I would turn their property into a first-class office building. Then I outlined my plans, step by step. I was prepared, and it showed. It also landed me the deal. That's how deals get done.

Negotiating isn't about calling all the shots—it's about ability: the power to convince people to accept your ideas. Present your ideas in a way that won't intimidate them. Let them think the decision is theirs. Bulldozing people into accepting your ideas is a recipe for disaster.

I walked into one deal with an aggressive plan in my head, but had to change my strategy when I met the individual in charge, who came from a prominent family. He was insecure and unassuming, not at all the powerhouse type I had expected. So I immediately started thinking how I could build up his esteem enough to get him into the negotiating arena. I could tell that he would walk away to avoid confrontation. I gained his confidence by building up his self-esteem.

Sometimes, you have to be a psychologist to figure out the best approach. Sometimes you have to be stubborn. Sometimes you have to be a chameleon and change your mind. What I'm saying is: Don't limit yourself.

Learn to balance passion with reason; you need both to negotiate successfully. Passion gets your adrenaline going, but reason keeps you on track.

LISTEN TO YOUR GUT

We all have instincts—the important thing is to know how to use them.

Knowing how to use your instincts is a mystery, even to those with sharp business skills. Some instincts you can't explain, but there are signs that can guide you to—or away from—certain people and certain deals.

Within a few seconds of meeting Mark Burnett, the creator of *The Apprentice*, I liked him, both as a person and as a professional. At other times, I've met people that I dislike for no particular reason. I try not to be judgmental, but I've learned to trust my gut and steer clear.

How do you learn how to do that? Tune in.

Have you noticed when you're in a situation that produces heightened alertness, how careful you are about what you say or do? Those are your instincts working for you. Trust them. Together, logic and instincts will help you make the best decisions.

When I first started building golf courses, my instincts told me it was a good business decision. I knew that if I combined my passion for golf with my knowledge of the process, I would succeed. So I found the best golf course designers in the world and spent many hours working with them. The results have been spectacular because I paired instinct and logic.

Spend some time with this innate aspect of yourself. Learning how to handle your instincts can give you an edge in many situations, business or otherwise. There are many things we can't see or hear; that is when we need to use our instincts to guide us.

Listen to your gut, and you will always have a reliable guide!

ENJOY COMPETITION

I like competition. I think it's healthy.

On July 12, 2005, I broke ground for the Trump International Hotel & Tower in Las Vegas. Starting a new building is always a big deal, but this one was particularly special. It was my first real estate venture in that town, and the fulfillment of a longtime dream.

Adding to the drama was the fact that the building is right across the road from Wynn Las Vegas, the signature property of my one-time nemesis, Steve Wynn, who reinvented the Strip with such mega resorts as The Mirage, Treasure Island, and the Bellagio.

Steve Wynn and I go way back. We squared off over the Hilton properties in Atlantic City back in the 1980s. Both of us have always built big, and we have the egos to match. With us, it used to be like the old Western stand-off, "This town's not big enough for the both of us." Now we're good friends. Back in the day, though, the competition was fierce—and I loved our battles.

Competition fires me up.

Competition pushes me to expand and extend my efforts beyond what I thought was possible.

Competition forces me to outdo myself. I love competition because, ultimately, it makes me bigger.

BE YOUR OWN BEST ASSET

Being a brand might sound complex to you, but it's not. Being a brand simply means that you are your own best asset. I never planned on becoming a brand, but, given my ideas, my aesthetic, and the circumstances that led to an expanding network of interests, "Trump" has become a great brand that delivers luxury and exclusivity.

It all started with Trump Tower, my signature building that serves as the model for my brand. People pay more to live in or rent space in my buildings because of the association with me and my ideals. These ideals are constantly put into practice in ways both big and small, such as the illuminated seven-story waterfall cascading over finely matched Italian marble in the atrium of Trump Tower.

I avoid the commonplace and give tenants and buyers more than they might expect. That's a big part of the Trump brand. Become your own best asset and adopt the mentality of an investor. Make decisions and take or delegate actions now that will bear fruit later. That's the key to wealth creation. Don't jump at the best offers, or slap your name on anything you think people might buy. Believe in whatever you put your name on, and make sure it reflects who you truly are.

GET GOING!

Are you ready for the challenge of creating and building unlimited wealth? You've got work to do—work that's going to teach you how to create and build the wealth you want!

2

DEVELOP A MINDSET
FOR SUCCESS*
by
Marshall Sylver

Do you think that it is possible for you to be a millionaire? Do you believe that there are a million ways to be a millionaire? My guess is that you do. So if that's true, then the only reason you aren't a millionaire is—you!

I want to help you change from the inside out so you can think about creating wealth the way a millionaire does.

Rich people think differently than poor people. I'm not talking about rich people who earn a million dollars or more a year by working 70 and 80 hours a week, sacrificing their family, their health, and their well-being in the process, all in pursuit of the Almighty Dollar. I'm talking about earning money joyfully. Wouldn't that be wonderful, living a life that joyfully creates wealth?

---

*This material has been condensed from *What Would a Billionaire Do?* by Marshall Sylver. Copyright © pending. Used with permission. Any other use, please contact www.sylver.com.

The right financial habits can help you do that. In my seminars, I teach a technique I developed called "Psycho Neuro Duplication." Simply put, by thinking the way someone successful thinks, and then doing what they do, you will produce a similar result. It's a simple process, but one that demands discipline. When you think the way an active, fit person thinks and then do what they do, you'll become active and fit, too. It's the same with the financial habits that can make you wealthy.

By my definition, anyone who isn't earning a million dollars a year joyfully is a pauper. If hearing that makes you uneasy, or even angry, I'm glad. That reaction may push you to change your beliefs and actions so you finally can stop struggling with money. I can almost hear you saying, "That's easy for you to say, Marshall, as you drive around in your Rolls Royce and fly in a private jet. You don't know what it's like to be kicked out of your apartment for not being able to pay the rent."

Actually, I do know what it's like, which is why I'm the perfect person to teach you about wealth. I was born and raised on a farm in Michigan with no running water, no electricity, and often, little, and sometimes, no food. After my first home was condemned, my second home was a converted chicken coop. Other than making me very grateful for my humble roots, the only other side effect is that I tend to cluck when I get nervous (only kidding!).

My humble beginnings helped me see things differently. At the age of seven, I saw quite clearly that we were the poorest family in my community. Everyone else had more than my family, and many families made a lot of money. I knew they weren't smarter than me, or more creative, harder working, or better looking. I saw that they did things differently. They held different beliefs about life, and they took different actions. The biggest difference? They focused on making money, not holding onto it so tightly out of fear of the unknown.

If all of the money in the world was divided evenly among all of the people, within five years it would be right back in the same hands again. Why? People who know how to make money would keep making money, and hardworking, positive, motivated, intelligent people would stay poor, and for the same reason—because of their habits. They would simply squander the extra money and end up where they started. This is the reason so many people who receive a windfall of cash end up worse off than before they received it. They simply don't know how to live wealthy.

Let's start talking about how you can change the habits that keep you poor and, instead, adopt the "millionaire mindset" that will transform your life and make you wealthy. There are three big differences.

DIFFERENCE 1: MILLIONAIRES ELIMINATE MINIMUM WAGE ACTIVITIES FROM THEIR LIVES

As long as you fill up your day with minimum wage activities, it's not possible to be a millionaire. Do you take out your own trash? Pick up around the house? Do your own laundry? If you answered "Yes!" to any of those questions, then you're involved in minimum wage activities. If you want to generate a million dollars, or more, in revenue every year, then you must recognize that money is math. To do that, joyfully or otherwise, based on a 40-hour work week, 50 weeks a year, your time is worth $500 an hour minimum. Any action someone else can do for less doesn't fit millionaire habits.

See which minimum wage activities you can eliminate from your life. Start looking at more efficient ways to live your life and take action.

For example, do you spend two hours arguing about a cell phone bill because the phone company overcharged you $10? If you do, you'll never be a millionaire because, even if you win, you only made $5 an hour from that discussion. You may say, "Well, it's the principle." The principle is: you are struggling and you don't deserve to struggle. Would a millionaire spend two hours a night watching cable television? Probably not—unless they owned the network! Millionaires consistently ask themselves, "What is the highest and best use of my time?"

Abraham Lincoln said that if you have one hour to chop down a tree, spend 40 minutes sharpening the ax. You could chop down the tree by hitting it with a dull ax. The tree may fall after an hour, the challenge is your hands will be bruised and blistered and you won't be able to chop down the next tree. If, however, you spend 40 minutes sharpening that ax, in the next 20 minutes, you can chop down the tree with little effort. In fact, because you sharpened the ax and did the foundational work in the beginning, you then can chop down the next tree, and the next, and the next.

Letting go of instantaneous gratification is the lesson here, and in the long run it creates wealth. If you work 40, 50, and even 60 hours per week and come home at night exhausted, you can't afford cable TV. I'm not talking about the monthly fee; you can't afford spending those two hours watching TV when you could spend them sharpening your "ax."

You may be uncomfortable at first, yet remember the principle: Money is math. You have the same hours in your day as a millionaire or billionaire who knows how to best utilize their time and resources. You'll begin to grow to a place where you no longer have to trade hours for dollars.

Like me, you were probably raised by parents who wanted you to have a better life, but may not have motivated you in ways that were successful.

When I was growing up, my mother would tell me, "Marshall, work hard, get ahead," and she meant well, yet her mindset hindered my life for years. This angel on earth raised 10 children, largely on her own, and worked three jobs to put food on the table for us, yet her idea of creating greater wealth was to sleep one hour less so that she could work one more hour.

For years, I traded my precious hours for too few dollars. I was always asking myself, "how can I get more work done?" and always struggling, until one day when I was in my early twenties. I was searching frantically for enough spare change in the couch to buy a box of macaroni and cheese. I was about to be kicked out of my apartment for nonpayment of the rent and I was the manager! I realized I had to start clearing my mind of the pauper thoughts that were holding me captive. I started asking, "How can I create more wealth?" and as I did, I began to see a second big difference between millionaires and paupers.

DIFFERENCE 2: MILLIONAIRES UPGRADE THE VALUE OF THEIR TIME

What do you think is more valuable, a Moped or a Rolls Royce? A Rolls Royce, of course—unless you live on a mountain with goat paths for roads. Then, a Moped is far more valuable. What I'm saying is, what something costs has nothing to do with its value; it's what others are willing to pay that matters.

You are rewarded in life by what you create as value for someone else. Look at all the new service businesses and products we have today that didn't exist 20, 10, or even 5 years ago. Could you have ever imagined that someday, you might pay a "pet-sitter," while you were at work or on vacation? Spend $5 for a cup of coffee, or $1 for a bottle of water? Use a "sponge-less" mop to clean up a spill? How many times have you seen a product advertised on television or in a store and thought: "I wish I had come up with that idea. What a timesaver!" You can create value for others with the most common, or most exotic, idea or concept.

To create wealth, you also have to upgrade the value of your time so that others are willing to pay more for it. How do you do that? Give more than you ask. Remember that those who receive what you create determine its value. If you had paid every dollar you have to buy this book, you would be reading it more thoughtfully. When this information multiplies your net worth 1,000 times over, it is worth every dollar.

Difference 3: Millionaires Never Ask "How *Much* does it Cost?"; Millionaires Ask "How *Much* Will it Make Me?"

As a millionaire, I know that I have to take risks to create wealth; I must put my money, my reputation, and my talents on the line. Millionaires constantly look at the upside and seldom focus on the downside. If something costs me $1 million to buy, yet earns me $1.5 million, cost is irrelevant.

Paupers are always concerned with cost because they have a very limited view of what is possible. How much faith and follow-through are you willing to give to launching your own business?

To be an entrepreneur means you will be moving ahead without clear direction, and often in the face of fear. When everyone else gives up, you have the energy and enough belief in yourself to keep going. You understand your customers because you work hard at understanding what they want. You are confident about your goal; as a result, others will follow you because they want to share the faith and adventure you instill in them. For you to be able to lead and persuade others toward your vision, you must possess the three specific skills discussed next.

Skill 1: Control Your Thoughts and Emotions

You may already have a good idea of how wealthy people—athletes, entertainers, and real estate tycoons—make millions of dollars joyfully every year, so there are only two reasons why you don't have what you want right now: either you don't know the ABC's of making your dreams come true, or, if you do, you won't get off the couch to take consistent action on a regular basis.

Want to lose weight? After years of study, scientific research, thousands of examples, and cases of people who were successful at taking the fat off of their bodies that they wanted to take off, we have come up with a powerful formula that works every single time: Eat Less—Move More!

Want to make more money naturally? Apply the same thinking: Work Less—Add More Value!

What if how you lived your life on a daily basis brought great joy to you? What if what you *thought* created wealth and attracted financial security to you? In this chapter, start thinking like a millionaire—even if the money hasn't been deposited into your bank account yet.

Skill 2: Use the Right Tools

Learning to sell and market your idea is critical. By having the right tools, you understand the processes that others have used to create wealth, and you use them for yourself. For specifics on the hands-on tools you'll need, check out Part IV of this book, *Be the Boss: The Entrepreneur's Path to Wealth*. Most companies are started by people who figured out how to "build a better mousetrap." Leverage a great idea or create your own—it doesn't matter. Figure out how to do a business better; that's the path to wealth.

Skill 3: Take Action in the Present Moment

When? Right now. "Tomorrow" never comes. What you don't do in this moment, most likely you'll never do at all. If you're like most people, if you don't exercise in the morning, chances are you won't as the day's demands and distractions mount up. That's unfortunate, because what keeps you healthy and on track should be the highest priority of your day, not the lowest. Do yourself a favor and circle the word "Action" in the heading.

No risk, no goodies. Millionaires know that at times, they have to "fail forward fast" to become wealthy. They know that not all seeds fall on fertile soil; that's just part of the game.

If you've ever played Monopoly, you know that there's a very specific strategy to winning: you buy every single property you land on. Do that, and halfway through the game, you'll run out of money. It looks like other people, who have more money than you, are winning. To buy more property, you now have to borrow against your existing properties, often reaping half their value and paying high interest. But when everyone runs out of property, you're able to cash in because your properties are now income-generating assets. By playing with that strategy, you'll always win.

Such thoughts are common to a millionaire's mindset. You'll begin to notice that paupers jump on the stock market, real estate, or business band-wagon, when rich people are jumping off with their profits. Buy low, sell high. Buy when everyone is selling. Leverage other people's creativity. To become a shepherd, do the exact opposite of what the sheep are doing.

One day, while I was scrounging in the couch for enough money to buy macaroni and cheese, I finally said out loud, "I want a different life," and started controlling my pauper thoughts.

To become successful, I had to learn to eliminate these two pauper mental thoughts:

"Wealthy people must be doing something illegal, immoral, or unethical, etc. It's so easy for them to make money, and so difficult for me."

Millionaires do what they love, they do it often, and they get better and better as a result. For example, I have always loved to be on stage, to perform, and to share with others what I learn. Am I good at performing because I enjoy it, or do I enjoy performing because I'm good at it? It doesn't matter, as long as the common denominator is enjoyment, and I follow what is in my heart and what makes me happy. Doing what you love, though, isn't always easy, and success is not a one-time achievement. I am constantly seeking more information and more knowledge to bring more value to my audience. Pauper thoughts number two:

"Don't sell me anything. If you do, I'll lose."

Paupers are afraid to invest in their dreams. Millionaires know that the more cash flows, the more cash there is for everyone.

After the terrorist attacks on 9/11, our political leaders delivered the right advice to a grieving American people: Our economy is in peril. If you want to help, go out and buy your kids the school clothes you were thinking of buying. Go out and buy that new car. Upgrade your home. Why? Because as long as money is flowing, our economy is sound. It's the same dynamic with your own personal economy. To increase financial awareness and abundance, plant seeds in places where they can grow. My good friend, the investor and best-selling author Robert Kiyosaki, says you should always invest in income-generating assets. Paupers hear that and say, "I'll only invest in real estate because that shows an immediate return." That's not what Robert is saying.

Buy whatever you want and make it make you money.

One of my students, Jerry Arrola, had a water company that he sold at a great profit and then retired. Since his time in the military service, he liked flying helicopters, so he bought one, quickly upgraded to another . . . and another, until his wife told him to stop buying "toys"; he was wasting their money. Instead of getting rid of his helicopters, Jerry, who has a millionaire mindset, told himself, "I'm going to have my toys make me money." He now owns the largest helicopter-training facility in the world. Headquartered in

Nevada, with facilities in 15 states, Silver State Helicopters generates over $100 million a year in revenue. Jerry bought what he wanted and turned it into an income-generating asset.

Millionaires buy what they want and then figure out how to use that purchase to make money. Are you holding on too tightly to your current assets?

By increasing your ability to risk, you get more in return. The great hockey player Wayne Gretzky put it this way: "You miss every shot you don't take."

Recently, I had the great fortune to dine with rebel billionaire Richard Branson, who founded Virgin Atlantic Airways. Faced with a decision to sell his beloved airline and walk away with half a billion dollars—he put it all back on the table and leveraged many billions more to start new businesses, including travel into outer space.

Ask yourself today: What would a millionaire do right now? Spend two hours arguing about a cell phone bill? Get stressed because they didn't get a decent raise? No! They would ask their boss, "How can I be in business with you?" or, better yet, ask, "How can I start or buy my own business?" It's time to unleash the millionaire in you.

3

LEARN MILLIONAIRE HABITS*

by

Marshall Sylver

Real estate won't make you wealthy, the Internet doesn't print cash, and the stock market can't make you rich. *You* make you rich; more specifically, your habits make you rich. There's no way around it: your habits either make you or break you. You will have either discipline or regrets.

All happy, healthy, and wealthy people develop and master five key personal habits:

1. Spiritual health.
2. Balance.
3. Priority management.
4. Great vision.
5. Plan setting.

---

*This material has been condensed from *A Wallet Once Expanded*, by Marshall Sylver. Copyright © pending. Used with permission. Any other use, please contact www.sylver.com.

I emphasize "happy and healthy" for a reason. I wouldn't dream of teaching you how to make money without helping you to establish the proper foundation that allows you to enjoy your wealth. Learn and master these millionaire habits, and you'll be able to capitalize on the wealth-building vehicles described throughout this book. If you don't—you'll have regrets later, and wish you had.

Let's look at the first successful habit, and the true foundation of all wealth.

SPIRITUAL HEALTH

If you think being poor is tough, try being rich without being spiritually centered. Spiritual health is understanding that, ultimately, all of the money in the world isn't going to make you happy. If you don't like yourself when you're poor, you sure won't like yourself when you're rich; in fact, money makes the struggle harder.

That's why it's important to find a spiritual path that works for you. Finding wealth without finding peace is setting yourself up for disaster. Money can create paranoia, distance you from the people you love, and stimulate and create addictions. Wealth gives you enough money to indulge yourself with harmful things like drugs, alcohol, greed, and worse. Instead, armed with a spiritual discipline, you'll be able to do the effective thing, and do it daily so you can learn to truly love yourself and be freed up to do good work. There really is no right or wrong, just consequences.

Spiritual health starts with the knowledge that the size of your bank account doesn't dictate your self-worth. By truly liking who you are—with or without money—you'll make much better judgments and not get bogged down in emotional quicksand. In the course of building a successful business, it's normal to have setbacks. There will be bumps in the road—that is guaranteed. By being spiritually healthy, you'll be secure in your own identity and more willing to take calculated risks that are the foundation of creating wealth.

Spiritual health keeps you clear minded and joyful and free of worry about the future. It also gives a strong moral foundation to enjoy your wealth. Ever wonder why the rich get richer? Because they have a spirit of gratitude. They're grateful for what they have. And this spirit of gratitude allows them to look for what is working every day. We always find what we are looking for. What we focus on expands. This mindset allows you to constantly deal with what emerges and to find it not only useful, but actually perfect.

BALANCE

I wouldn't dream of teaching you how to create wealth without teaching you how to create balance first. Money without balance is the surest way down that slippery slope to a living hell.

You need to create and maintain mental, physical, relational, and then financial balance. When your priorities are in order, wealth will come easily and readily to you. You'll be happier and much more effective.

Notice the order I laid out: mental, physical, relational, and *then* financial. Most people reverse the order.

Balance begins with good mental health, otherwise the battle to create wealth is nearly impossible. Paying attention to your mental "diet" shapes your ability to succeed. Just as junk food makes the body sluggish, feeding your mind "junk food" makes your mind sluggish, too. Millionaires and successful entrepreneurs pay close attention to what they read. Most read and study the biographies of people who have succeeded before them, and avoid reading the newspaper every day, since much of the news is sensationalized and filled with gossip. Focus your reading on content that is positive, uplifting, and teaches you something useful.

Since your thoughts create your emotions, taking control of your thoughts automatically allows you to respond rather than to react. Instead, your needs now become your desires; this allows you to do what's most effective, rather than to react because you feel your rights have been violated. Having "rights" sets you up to be wronged. In the world of making money, you may often be offended. Surrender to the fact that business isn't fair. Once you accept that, you won't experience the emotional charge you get from feeling that someone took advantage of you. You will simply learn the lesson and move on.

Balance means you understand that time spent with family, time spent contributing to your community, and time spent with your "higher power" are all essential to creating not only wealth, but also satisfaction.

I travel a great deal, and realize that the most valuable asset I have is my time, not just as it relates to generating income, but also because it cuts into the time I am able to spend maintaining the balance for which I strive. For these reasons, I gave up flying on commercial airlines a long time ago. On any given trip, I spent three and a half hours extra flying through a commercial airport, rather than one of the 5,000 regional airports that are usually 15 minutes away from anybody's home. I had to park my car, get in line with hundreds, even thousands, of other travelers, go through security, reach the gate, and then pray that my flight would be on time. Once I finally deplaned, I had to wait for my baggage, which was sometimes delayed by 45 to 60 minutes, before I was able to head toward my final destination—only to repeat this process on the way home. That averaged seven extra hours each time I traveled.

By flying privately, I now drive seven minutes from my home to the nearest airport. I pull my car up to my jet, my pilot unloads my baggage from the trunk and transfers it to the plane, and I get on board. I'm in the air and on my way to my destination within 15 minutes of leaving my home. When I land, I repeat the process. If I travel only twice a week, then I add 14 hours to my ability to maintain balance and increase productivity. Can you imagine how much more inspired you can be when you don't have to suffer the anxiety of commercial travel? Mastering this next habit helped me increase my Work-Life Balance.

PRIORITY MANAGEMENT

If you're always working and not getting ahead, you're getting the wrong things done first. Millionaires tackle head-on what I call the "Worst Things First List"; those tasks the ordinary person puts off that, ironically, most need to get done. Remember that millionaires earn $1 million a year joyfully. Paupers (those earning less than $1 million a year) are constantly busy doing busy things, and never accomplishing anything of value. Do not mistake action for accomplishment.

I teach students in my Millionaire Mentorship Program to control their priorities. Priority management teaches you to maintain balance in your life, so you don't jeopardize your health or relationships. You cannot control or even manage time; you can only manage what is most important—your priorities. I tell my students to plan their entire day in advance for maximum productivity, to accomplish their most important priorities first. If they run out of time at the end of the day, the priorities that get put off are the ones of least importance.

Priority management is also the key that unlocks creative thinking that generates wealth. Contrary to what some think, creativity doesn't happen in a sudden burst of inspiration; it is a disciplined process that achieves results by focusing on a specific outcome.

Creative people, who become wealthy people, get more done in less time because they manage time in a planned, effective order. They focus their time on creating something new or innovative. I speak from my own experience. I do my best creative thinking after my workouts. My endorphin levels are high. My confidence is up because I have just done something good for myself. Therefore, after working out in the morning, I schedule one hour to focus only on creativity. I turn off my cell phone, e-mail, and instant messaging programs, and tell anyone who interrupts that I'm focusing on a creative project and will get back to them in an hour.

Try this for 21 days, and see what happens.

GREAT VISION

Do what you love and the money will follow: Focus on being the best at something and there will always be a market for your goods and services.

This lesson will help you see beyond the challenges and think big. Small plans equal small motivations. People who create wealth are just like you, with one exception—they have more clarity of vision, and they're much more excited about their future. Napoleon Hill, in his scholarly work, *Think and Grow Rich* (New York, Random House, 2002) defines purpose: Knowing what your final outcome is in advance, seeing the successful completion of your objectives, and being confident about its successful completion. By being secure in what you're doing, and where you're going, the inevitable trials and tribulations along the way become manageable, and even exciting.

The theory of relativity wasn't created on a blackboard; it was created when Albert Einstein imagined himself on the tip of a beam of light traveling through space. Walt Disney created the term "imagineering" to describe the building of his dreams. Donald J. Trump doesn't look at a piece of undeveloped land and see dirt; he sees a beautiful building or development, and people in a bidding war for the privilege of owning a piece.

Great vision is the ability to see things before they happen. Millionaires almost always speak in the future tense. They speak of the projects as if they are already completed because, in their mind, they are. I call this process of projection, *entrepreneurial exaggeration*. The entrepreneur isn't lying, rather believes with all their heart and soul that what they set out to accomplish is already done. They are doing the very thing that is the foundation of all great things; they are projecting forward. Show me someone who knows where he or she is going, and I promise you—everyone will want to come along.

PLAN SETTING

What's the difference between a person whose dreams remain just dreams and someone who gets things done? Planning. I teach people in my seminars to remove the word *goal* from their vocabulary. Since your subconscious computer (your subconscious mind) will only produce exactly what you tell it to, aiming for a goal is very different than executing a plan. You don't need to know every step to start. Whatever you envision right now, whatever you aspire to in this moment, you already have some of the elements in hand. Take the first step, and the next step will become clear.

Put your vision on paper. Grab a pen and piece of paper and describe your perfect working day, from the moment you wake up to the moment you go to sleep. With whom do you interact? Who is on your team? How much money do you make from your activities? What great fun do you have?

By doing that, you take the first step toward making that mental picture a reality. Once you do, you can start to break it down into doable steps.

Here are the basic elements of plan setting:

- *Plan high.* Small plans do not inspire. Big plans make you passionate. Most people are playing a small game, and produce small results. John D. Rockefeller said, "Play with pennies, you make pennies. Play with dollars, you make dollars." Worst case scenario: You accomplish only part of your plan. You wanted to become a billionaire, and you only became a multimillionaire instead. Poor baby!
- *Chunk it down.* Take small steps. Even if it's not all doable right now, some is. A steady and certain march toward your plan will get you further than you realize. Critical mass takes over at some point, and all the things you have done suddenly add up. Looking at the big picture of anything can be overwhelming, so when you feel a task is too big, ask yourself this question. Post it near your workspace, so you can refer to it whenever you feel stuck.

"What is powerful, productive, positive, and leads me toward what I am working on? Do it now!"

- *Action versus production quotas.* In the beginning of any game, it's important to set yourself up to win. List what you will do, instead of what you will accomplish. Calling 10 potential customers in one hour is an action quota, closing three new sales is a production quota. You don't need to lose 10 pounds, you need to get to the gym every day. The fat comes off when you take action. Taking consistent, powerful, productive action in the present moment will always move you closer to what you want.

- *Personal alterations.* What is stopping you from getting what you want? Who you are always determines what you get. Something about you, and something that you consistently do, has been stopping you from living the life you deserve. What personal habit is standing in your way? Procrastination? Complacency? Pride? Ego? Take a personal inventory, and make a plan for change. If you can't figure this out, you are in denial. Truly effective millionaires and billionaires can easily tell you what they need to change to make themselves more effective. It's called self-awareness. Become self-aware, and every change becomes obvious. Challenge yourself and complete Exhibit 3.1. To download your

Downloadable Exhibit 3.1 Millionaire Mindset and Habits Worksheet*

What truly brings you joy? _____

Can you envision doing these activities every day? _____

What research will help you take the next step? _____

Are you living in the present moment? _____

Are you truly grateful for who and what, you have in your life? _____

Do you have habits that are blocking you from what you want? _____

Are you the best at what you do? _____

What seminars, books, or other resources should you seek? _____

Are you up to date with the latest technology and trends in your industry? _____

Do you read relevant material about your industry every day? _____

Do you plan your day in advance? _____

Do you procrastinate about important tasks and do the easy ones first? _____

Do you spend some of your downtime on unproductive activities that do not contribute to producing wealth? _____

Do you have a clear, definitive picture of your vision? _____

Do you spend time describing it, visualizing it, and filling in all of the details? _____

**Note:* A blank version of this exhibit can be downloaded from www.trumpuniversity.com/wealthbuilding101 for your personal use.

Millionaire Mindset and Habits Worksheet, visit www.trumpuniversity.
com/wealthbuilding101.
- *Read your plan every day.* Make it an obsession. Post pictures, draw-
ings, and reminders everywhere you turn, so you become what you
plan: successful. Taste it, see it, feel it. Let it become your reality
before the world even thinks it is a possibility. Start "acting as if" it is
already true, and you will attract the people you need to accomplish it.

Millionaires and billionaires are constantly feeding their minds with
healthy information. Like any muscle, the mind needs to exercise or it will
die. Reading is one way to stimulate your mind "muscle," because it requires
you to be active instead of passive. Reading every day also can improve the
way you communicate. Not only will your vocabulary increase, but also biographies will reveal how successful people became wealthy due in part to their
ability to communicate. Great businesspeople like Donald J. Trump or Mark
Cuban, or many other millionaires or billionaires, are also great communica-
tors. The wealthiest man on the planet, Bill Gates, has an incredible ability
to communicate his ideas, his creativity, and his motivation to other people to
inspire them to be more than they thought they could be.

Communication equals wealth. The quality of our lives is the quality of our
communication, both with ourselves and with the outside world. Communication with ourselves is a form of *programming*. It's the 1,500 words per minute
whizzing through our brain that tell us who we are, or are not; what we can
be, or not be; what we can do, or not do; and what we can have, or not have.
Communication with the outside world is called *influence*. Influence is not the
ability to get somebody else to say yes to what you are offering. True influence is the ability to persuade somebody else to ask for what you are selling
and have them believe it was their idea.

I have made millions of dollars by helping others get what they want.
The challenge is: Most people don't know what they want until you tell them.
I call the process of influencing other people to ask for what you are selling
the *persuasion equation*.

There are five steps:

1. *Gain rapport and trust.* We don't buy anything at any price from someone we don't trust.
2. *Elicit the buyer's outcome.* Your job as a master influencer is to make
what you are selling look like what the other person wants.

3. *Give the buyer a directive to take the action steps necessary to get what he or she wants.* Other people need permission, and seek validation, to take the actions that will get them what they seek.

4. *If they resist, give more information.* The only reason a person says no to a directive is that they fear a loss. Influence is playing with the buyer's resistance, and knowing that is all part of the process. On average, people say no five times before they say yes.

5. *Give the directive to take action again.*

Repeat Steps 4 and 5 until you reach your outcome: influencing the other party.

Being an effective communicator both internally and externally requires practice. It is a learned skill set, and does not happen naturally. For more information, I suggest you read one of the best books ever written—mine—on the subject, *Passion, Profit and Power* (New York: Simon & Schuster, 1995). It was a glorious day for fools when modesty became a virtue, don't you agree?

Right now you're faced with the decision to move ahead or stay stuck where you are. In the movie, *The Shawshank Redemption*, Andy Dufresne says, "Get busy living, or get busy dying." So what are you gonna do? Make a commitment today to apply and master the habits of wealthy people described in this chapter and you'll be ready to use the wealth-building strategies my colleagues share throughout this book.

The truth is: you've never been comfortable being a pauper; it's not your natural state. You're a millionaire. The money may not have been deposited in your bank account, yet it's still who you are. Don't wait for the world's validation; know it is your soul. Whether it's a better car, house, or lifestyle, a life once expanded never contracts. Once you get accustomed to living in a more effective, more powerful and passionate way, I promise, you'll never go back to your old life. In fact, you'll smile and ask, "What took me so long?"

Here's to looking out the window of my private jet, and seeing you wave back through the window of yours!

II

Plan Smart:
Your Playbook for
Financial Success

4

WRITE YOUR FINANCIAL
VISION STATEMENT
by
John R. Burley

Y ou might be surprised to learn that one of the most powerful habits of
wealthy people is their ability to visualize a better financial future. They
develop a clear mental picture of where they want to be financially, and then
describe their financial vision in a simple and concise statement to serve as a
constant reminder of where they are headed. This picture becomes a powerful motivator in their quest to produce and acquire wealth.

If you can get a clear picture of the way you want your life to look, that
glimpse, quite often, may be enough to keep you moving ahead in pursuit of
your personal dream.

Sadly, many people don't pursue their dreams. Wise and wealthy King
Solomon wrote, "Where there is no vision, the people perish." He understood that once people lose their vision of a better future, they lose their
hope—and even their desire—to persevere through life's challenges. Many
people have some idea of what they would like their ideal lives to look like,
but they convince themselves that dreams never come true. The truth is, most

people could fulfill their dreams, and make their lives better, if they would only take some time to define a plan of action and follow their plan by developing a financial vision statement.

Say you spend $900 a month servicing debt and, in 18 months, you reach your goal of becoming debt-free. Your goal is to get out of debt, but your vision is much bigger. As you keep moving ahead, you are pursuing a vision of what life will be like once you reach your goal. You can, and should, enjoy the feeling of having the burden of debt lifted off your shoulders, but thinking about how to invest some of the money you saved is what keeps you moving ahead. Do you see the difference between a financial goal and a financial vision? A goal is a measurable step, while a vision is a picture of the future you can achieve once the goal is reached.

So start thinking about your financial vision statement. Get in touch with what you truly want out of life. Then work through these five simple steps to develop a financial vision statement that can guide you to create wealth.

Visualize Your Ideal Life

Take some time to paint a word picture of the life you want to live. Take a piece of paper and sit down in a quiet spot. Write out a schedule for your ideal day. What would you do each morning? Begin with some time at the gym, or a leisurely coffee at your favorite bistro? Maybe on your ideal day, you hike on your favorite trail, or row a kayak across a lake. What would you do each afternoon? Each evening? I'm not talking about how you would spend your ideal vacation day, but a typical day of your ideal life. Your vision might include frequent travel to exotic and adventurous locations, but what would your ideal day look like when you are home? Where would you be living? Perhaps in the same town, but in a different home, or you might choose to move to a totally different location or community. As you begin to visualize the ideal life you would like to live, don't be afraid to dream big. Be realistic, but don't limit yourself; this vision will form the foundation of the financial goals you will set and the investing strategies that you will use. Take some time to paint your mental picture by fantasizing about a typical day in your ideal life.

As a guide to get you started on this journey, answer these "vision-planting" questions:

What do I really want to accomplish with my life? What is my purpose?
What do I want spiritually?

What type of person do I want to be?

Where do I want to live? Who do I want in my life? What type of life-style do I want?

What have I always dreamed of doing? What big things do I want to accomplish in my life?

What "toys" would I like to have for my family and me?

What sort of money/income do I want to have/make?

Now put a place and a time on each of these questions, and the action steps you will need to take. Begin the process, and soon you will see amazing results. Do this now, so you can see what your life will look like in the future. To download your Financial Vision Statement (Exhibit 4.1), visit www.trumpuniversity.com/wealthbuilding101.

As you complete this exercise, you might feel the way you will when you are out of debt and in control of your time and energy—exhilarated,

Downloadable Exhibit 4.1 Your Financial Vision Statement*

What do I really want to accomplish with my life? What is my purpose?

Become fearless. Make $, buy freedom, travel, indulge.

What do I want spiritually?

Health, love, great relationship.

What type of person do I want to be?

Balanced
humble
rich
influential
free

Where do I want to live? Who do I want in my life? What type of lifestyle do I want?

NYC,

Family,

Not too busy,

What have I always dreamed of doing? What big things do I want to accomplish in my life?

What "toys" would I like to have for my family and me?

houses

cars

How much money/income do I want to have?

lots

Note: A blank version of this exhibit can be downloaded from www.trumpuniversity.com/ wealthbuilding101 for your personal use.

and excited. Let yourself experience that emotion. We human beings are very much motivated by the emotions we associate with our experiences. Enjoy the feeling of true freedom that comes from controlling the choices that shape your life.

Let me give you an example. Let's say that right now you are carrying more debt than you would like. There are certain things you would rather be doing with your life, but because of your debt load, you are trapped in an unsatisfying job and working for an unfriendly boss. At times, your debt is like a heavy weight holding you down. What would it feel like to be out from under that debt completely? What if you never had to go to that job again, or face that boss? How would you feel? Are you smiling? By doing this exercise and allowing yourself to feel the emotions of your ideal life, you are providing yourself with the powerful mental and emotional motivators to keep moving in the right direction.

Make sure you take some time to write down your answers to these questions. Keep them available and look at them often. You will be amazed at how energizing these statements can be as they remind you of what you are striving for. Be as detailed as you want to be at this point in your visioning process. After you have completed this step, you will then become more precise in your statements about your ideal life, but don't worry about precision right now. We will talk more about that in the next section.

Having a clear vision is key to building wealth. "Visioning" on a regular basis is one of the most powerful habits you can develop. Many of the most successful graduates of my "Advanced Investing Real Estate Boot Camp" regularly take some time out of their lives to sit and imagine what their lives will be like when they achieve their financial goals. They tape pictures to their bathroom mirrors of the places they want to visit, or the dream homes or cars they want to own. These pictures serve as visual reminders and focus their attention every day on the better life they want to live.

Highly successful people who realize their dreams and goals in life are usually singularly motivated by a vision of the way they want their lives to be. Take some time to develop the habit of visioning. It will keep you keep focused on why you are striving for change in the first place.

WRITE IT DOWN

Now, I want you to verbalize your vision statement in a sentence or two. Write it down. You want your financial vision statement to capture the essence of the visioning you did in the previous exercise. If your statement is simple and precise enough, it can become your mantra as you pursue your personal financial freedom. Repeat it to yourself regularly to stay on track.

Let me give you an example. Let's say you work too much, to the point where your schedule keeps you away from your spouse and children more than you would like. As you envision your ideal life, you decide that you want to pursue financial freedom and work as a private investor from home.

You visualize a home office with a big window that looks out into the backyard of a newer home in a nicer neighborhood. You see yourself driving your kids to school every morning, attending their soccer games and performances, and taking your family on day hikes on the weekends. That's what your ideal life looks like. How can you capture that grand vision in a concise statement that helps you stay focused on the financial freedom you need to live the life you want? You write:

> "I am becoming financially free so that I can spend quality time with my husband and children. I want to be able to spend my best waking hours with my family so we can pursue deeper relationships with one another."

In the first step, you painted a picture of your ideal life; now you are filling in the specifics as a compass to guide you in pursuit of your financial goals. Be as elaborate or as simple as you want to be in this step, but do it so that your wealth-building efforts have a sense of purpose.

REHEARSE YOUR TRUE PRIORITIES

As you went through the previous exercises and took stock of how you would organize your ideal day, you began to identify your true priorities. True priorities are what we value in life and are closely related to our vision of the life we want to live. It is possible that you have lost touch with your true priorities along the way.

If you haven't taken the time to define your priorities, sit down with a piece of paper and pen in hand, and make a list of what's most important in your life. You don't need to start from scratch to do this exercise. Assuming that you took me seriously and wrote down your vision of a better life and your concise personal financial vision statement, you already did the work. Now review what you wrote, and identify the elements of your financial vision that are most important to you in life. Don't worry about putting them in some kind of order—that's really not necessary. The key is identifying what's important.

Then put that list in a place where you will see it on a regular basis until you refine your priorities. Rehearsing your true priorities plays a powerful role in staying motivated. Take time each week to reflect and keep focused, so that you can keep moving in the right direction. Successful people keep their list close at hand, and rehearse their priorities regularly.

Make sure you pay attention and regularly rehearse your priorities.

BELIEVE IN YOURSELF

One of the most important habits to develop in building wealth is the ability to believe in yourself and your vision. Belief comes before action. People take steps to make positive changes, because they believe their actions will produce great results.

Successful people believe in themselves and their vision. Donald J. Trump believed he could amass a personal fortune by developing high-end, exclusive properties. Berkshire Hathaway founder Warren Buffett believed he could turn $500 into a personal fortune, and he has. (He is now worth more than $40 billion.) As you take steps to build wealth, believe in yourself. Believe that what you are doing is good. Believe that you can build a better life—for yourself and others. Believe that your financial vision is worth pursuing, and believe that it is possible.

SURROUND YOURSELF WITH SUPPORTIVE PEOPLE

Successful people also know that a critical part of their success involves building a support network of people who will encourage them as they pursue their vision. Let me explain.

Our peers have a great deal of influence over us. Many people get sidetracked before they ever start moving down the path to a better life because they make the mistake of putting too much stock in the advice of unsuccessful people.

Often when a person makes a major change in life, they unavoidably find themselves surrounded by people who don't understand the inner transformation process or support the positive changes a person is trying to make in his life. Why are some people so critical and unsupportive? This is an incredibly complex question, but it's worth exploring for a moment.

Some people are naturally critical of people who are trying to make changes in their lives, because they don't want to admit to themselves that they are unhappy in their own circumstances. Deep down, they may envy your passion, and the courage that it takes to pursue something meaningful, but can't or won't admit that.

Another reason why some people are so unsupportive is *jealousy*, called the "green-eyed monster" by some because of the sheer ugliness it brings out in human relationships, along with its evil twin, envy. Jealousy is simply wishing that you had what someone else has. *Envy* is an advanced degree of jealousy, pushed to its most unhealthy extreme. When a person is jealous, he wishes that he had what his friend already has. When a person is envious, he also wishes that his friend didn't have it either.

Both emotions cause many people to be unsupportive of others who are trying to get more out of life. It's important to be aware of our own thoughts and actions, and those around us as we aspire for greater levels of success.

Don't be surprised when you realize that some people are unsupportive because they think your expectations are unrealistic. You can't expect people to feel the same intense passions about your personal growth and progress as you do; only you understand the intensity of your desire to pursue your vision. The antidote:

Intentionally seek out a handful of supportive people, or safe people, who can give you the encouragement and inspiration you need to move forward. That's why I created an online community of people at john burley.com. You are welcome to join our discussion forum, where you will find an entire community of likeminded people who support each other as they pursue and achieve financial excellence. Surrounding yourself with safe and supportive people is critical when you are making significant changes in your life. Positive people spur us on to believe in ourselves and take positive steps.

Grabbing hold of your vision is an exciting step toward becoming financially free. In the next chapter, we look at the financial habits that will help you achieve your vision. For more information, visit johnburley.com/trump.

5

CALCULATE WHAT
YOU NEED TO BECOME
FINANCIALLY FREE
by
John R. Burley

Our financial habits determine whether—or if—we will succeed. People with negative habits get negative results, while people with positive habits achieve positive results. That should be obvious, but I'm constantly amazed by people who have very negative, or even self-destructive, habits and then wonder why things don't work out.

In this chapter, I want to begin focusing your attention on the healthy financial habits you must develop to create wealth, which include eliminating debt, investing successfully, and contributing to charity. Without these habits, your biggest financial dreams will crumble and collapse.

First let's understand the nature of habits. Simply understood, habits are the routine behaviors that define what we do on a regular basis and dictate how we will react to any given situation. Surprisingly, new habits are easy to develop. Experts in human behavior tell us that if a person does something on a regular basis every day for 21 to 28 days, that person develops a habit. If a person exercises every morning for three to four weeks, then exercise becomes a habit for that person. If a person resolves to break a bad habit and sticks to that decision, the odds are very good that he or she will be able to overcome even the most harmful of habits—so be encouraged.

I want to help you develop the successful habits you need to become financially prosperous. Like every aspect of life, financial growth is a journey that begins with a clear understanding of where we are today, so we need to start with an honest assessment. When I plan a short trip, I often use mapquest.com. I enter my location, then my destination, and mapquest.com calculates the best route for me. In this chapter, we are going to do a financial mapquest search by entering our current financial location, and then taking the necessary steps to reach our destination.

The first step in this process is putting a price tag on the life you really want. It's reality-check time. I want to encourage you to take a close and honest look at where you are financially. Sit down with pen and paper. Ask yourself:

What will it take for me to become financially free?

Let me explain the question. Your ideal life comes with a certain price tag. In a capitalistic society, freedom costs money. To spend your time doing what you want, you will need to have a certain amount of money, or income stream, to pay for the financial lifestyle you want for you and your family. This is where the action begins. You need to get a very clear and honest picture of where you are financially, so that you can calculate how much money you will need to enjoy life and do what you want passionately to do.

Start with your monthly expenses. Then determine how much income you have, and how much you will need to replace, to become financially free. Take some time to figure this out. The numbers you plug into this calculation need to take into account everyone who depends on you. Exhibit 5.1 shows a partial list of the expenses you need to consider when determining your personal financial income. You can download your Personal Financial Statement at www.trumpuniversity.com/wealthbuilding101.

This last number may look intimidating, but remember, you need a clear and honest financial location, so you can reach your financial destination. The figure can be reached in a lump sum of capital, as demonstrated, or offset (that is, reduced) by other sources of income and/or reducing expenses (specifically debt). For most, this starting required capital will reduce as you take better control of your income and expense streams.

Downloadable Exhibit 5.1   Your Personal Monthly Financial Statement*

Fixed Expenses

Income tax	$_____
Home loan(s)	$_____
Car loan(s)	$_____
Personal loan(s)	$ _2,000_
Credit card(s) minimums	$_____
Property taxes	$_____
Insurances	$_____
Retirement contributions	$_____
Automatic Investment Plan	$_____
Debt reduction	$_____
Miscellaneous	$_____
Total	$_____

Variable Expenses

Food	$_____
Transportation	$_____
Clothing/personal care	$_____
Entertainment/holiday	$ _100_
Medical/dental	$_____
Utilities	$_____
Charitable giving	$_____
Miscellaneous	$_____
Total	$_____
Total Expenses	$ _100_

Now that you've added up your expenses, look at your current monthly income:

Income

Gross salary/wage	$ _5,280_
Interest/dividends	$_____
Commissions	$_____
Net rental income	$_____
Miscellaneous	$_____
Total	$ _5280_

(handwritten calculations: 400 x 6 2400. 10 x 8 80 80 320 2880 2400 5280)

How much income will you need to meet your expenses? Write down that number now.

Monthly income required _____

(Continued)

Downloadable Exhibit 5.1 (*Continued*)

Calculate how much money you will need annually to live the life you want. Multiply your monthly income required by 12:

Annual income required _____

Now multiply this annual figure by 10 (for the annual rate of return required), to produce the capital required. The objective here is to live off your investment income and not touch the principal.

Total investment capital _____

Note: A blank version of this exhibit can be downloaded from www.trumpuniversity.com/wealthbuilding101 for your personal use.

Controlling Debt

Now that you have some firm numbers in place, let's talk about the first financial habit that will help you to grow your numbers: controlling debt. I address specific strategies in the next chapter, but I want to talk about the many ways we fall into debt, often without realizing it. Realizing where you are, and how you got there, is the first step to heading in a new direction.

Once, several years ago, I was heavily in debt, with no light at the end of the tunnel. In fact, I believed I would be in debt for the rest of my life. I owed more than $20,000 on credit cards, my monthly car payments were over $1,000, and I owed more than $215,000 on my home. I made good money, but I didn't think I would ever dig out. As soon as I paid off one credit card balance, another expense would materialize. It was very frustrating and certainly depressing. The only way I would ever be able to pay off all my debt was to win the lottery or inherit money—but I didn't have any rich relatives. I share this with you not because I'm a rags-to-riches success story. I came from a middle-class family, and even though I always earned an above-average income, I often found myself buried in debt. I want those of you with debt issues to know that I understand, and care, because debt hits close to home with me. In the next section, "Act Now," I'm going to show you how to get out of debt—forever.

Many people find themselves in similar circumstances before they begin to take stock of their current financial situation. They struggle with the fact that the monthly payments just keep rising, bringing mounting pressure and stress.

It doesn't have to be that way for you. You can stop this bad habit right now. I did.

One day I sat down with my wife, Shari, and we set up a plan to systematically pay off all our debt. It took us a little over four years to become completely debt-free. (We have investment "debt," but that is intentional.) I can't describe how good it feels to go to sleep at night without owing other people money and worrying about bills. Our only monthly expenses are for utilities, food, insurance, and fun. (We place a lot of emphasis on fun.) The remainder of our income is ours to spend as we wish.

The sense of being free from the bondage of debt is truly exhilarating. Today, rather than struggling to stay ahead of monthly payments, we have the freedom to purchase what we want, and when we want it, on a cash basis.

Unfortunately, many people are drowning in a sea of financial despair. They've become slaves to their debt, and to the advertisers and banks that created this system of control. Advertisers have trained us to become voracious consumers who live and die by the motto: "Charge it!" "Buy it now!" "Do it now!" New plasma TV! New stereo! New bigger car! New boat! Great vacation! New house! The list goes on and on. Consume! Spend! Want!

Banks aren't any better. They want to separate you from as much of your hard-earned money as possible, which they accomplish by charging customers as many fees as possible, in small monthly payments until the day you die, and then beyond, collecting from your heirs if possible. They want you to be a debt slave to them for eternity. How do they do this? With that little piece of plastic called a credit card. With most credit cards, if you paid only the minimum monthly payment, you would spend close to four times more than what you actually paid for the original item. That's how credit cards are designed.

Don't get me wrong. I like buying and owning nice things, but the difference is, I pay in cash. I use an American Express card that I pay off at the end of each month, rather than carrying around actual cash. It's a good system that works for me. I don't accept monthly payment plans, and I don't spend beyond my means. The vast overwhelming majority of millionaires follow the same principles. I'm not a fanatical penny-pincher, and I'm not telling you to lower your standard of living. Far from it—I want you to actually increase your standard of living by making healthy and solid financial decisions. As you do, you'll be able to own the nice things you want by paying for them on a routine cash basis, instead of on a perpetual debt basis.

How do you make the transformation?

Say you purchase a new living-room set for $2,500, and the minimum monthly payment is $44.44 a month with an interest rate of 21 percent (which is normal for a furniture store charge card). At $44.44 a month, it would take you 20 years to pay for that set of living-room furniture. By the time you finish, you would have paid $10,665, rather than $2,500, because of all those small, silent, sneaky monthly payments.

Now let's look at the automobile industry. Say you're a 25-year-old female who leases a new car for $400 a month. You're thrilled to hear from the nice salesman that you can "rollover" your lease every two years and have a new car. Do you have any idea how much money you will spend during the next 40 years if you drive a new automobile every two to three years on lease? A whopping $417,867—for cars that you will never own. Don't believe me? Do the math: $400 a month for 40 years, with a car inflation index rate of 3.5 percent per year, totals $417,867. Want to lease a fancy luxury sedan or sports car? That $1,000-a-month lease will cost you more than $1 million!

Can you imagine paying more than $400,000 in small monthly car payments? It starts innocently enough, with an "offer" of a great rate or lease, but these companies aren't offering you the freedom to choose your lifestyle, but a one-way ticket to perpetual bondage. Companies train their salespeople so well that you slide into debt with a grateful smile on your face, and thank them for the ride.

For many, owning their own home is the biggest burden. Banks promote 30-year loans, knowing that the typical family moves every seven years or so. In the early years of the loan, most of the money paid goes to interest, not to principal. The longer the loan term, the more the amortization schedule works for the lender and against the consumer in the early years of the loan. For example, after seven years paying on a 30-year loan, most people will have paid down less than 7 percent of the principal on the house. Then it's time to get a new house or refinance and do it all again, if you follow the lender's plan.

When many homeowners sell their homes, they fall into a bigger trap by buying a bigger home, with a bigger mortgage, and start the whole "small payments" mentality all over again. My advice: Turn the amortization schedules in your favor by reducing the term of the loan, and increase the amount that goes toward paying off the principal. If you choose to pay off your mortgage over 15, instead of 30 years, you'll pay less interest from year one ($7,870 instead of $7,953). Your monthly payment will be higher ($955.65 versus $771.82, an extra $183.83 a month), but the average family can do it. It may sound incredible to you, but you can pay off all of your debts, including your house, in three to seven years. Don't expect most banks to offer you this information.

If at this point you feel discouraged, that's okay. You've worked on your vision statement, and taken a hard look at some initial numbers. Don't get hung up on the past. Now we're going to work together to improve what you are doing right, and fix what is broken. You've got your vision. Focus on that, and we will keep moving ahead. For more information, visit johnburley. com/trump.

6

DRAFT YOUR
FINANCIAL DREAM TEAM
by
John R. Burley

If you want to build rock-solid wealth, you need a team of trusted advisors to help you make decisions. I read voraciously, attend seminars and workshops, and have a vast base of real-world knowledge to draw on when making financial decisions. But I don't know everything. One of the smartest things I ever did in starting my business was to surround myself with a group of trusted advisors who are experts in their particular financial niches. In this chapter, I want to talk to you about what you need to keep in mind in building your own "dream team."

Let's start with financial advisors, and how you determine what you need. Many call themselves financial planners or advisors (which, by the way, in the United States requires no licensing or training), but unfortunately, they aren't; they're really just salespeople. How can you tell the difference? Let me explain.

Financial Planners Aren't Always What They're Cracked Up to Be

For many years, I was a financial planner who worked on commission sales. In every sales office where I worked, there was a board listing the name of each salesperson, along with his or her sales and earnings for the month.

Why I am telling you this? To impress on you what I learned by studying those boards: In commission sales, 5 percent of the salesforce is outstanding, 15 percent are very good (the top 20 percent earn 80 percent of all commissions), and 80 percent aren't good at all at sales (the 80 percent only make 20 percent of the commissions).

For several years, I worked in the top-producing office for the tenth largest financial planning company in the United States. There were almost 100 agents in the office, but less than five truly knew what they were doing. Another 10 or so were very good, but they worked on estate planning or business primarily, with only the wealthiest clients. Like myself, these top agents did not meet with the average person. Few of the other 80 or so agents lasted more than two to three years in the business. Most struggled to pay their own bills, and few offered advice that made their clients money (other than the luck of the market).

Agents were trained to focus on selling life insurance, then mutual funds. Why? Because the license to sell life insurance is the easiest one to get, and selling life insurance pays the highest commission, from 80 percent to 85 percent of the first year's premium. If your name was not at the top of the list on the sales board, and you were not selling life insurance, you could count on being called into the manager's office and read the riot act.

From my experience, I can tell you that the top 5 percent are truly outstanding. They invest themselves, are personally wealthy, and represent many high-end clients, but high-end planners work only for the wealthy. The next 15 percent of planners are great. They make solid decisions, provide above-average rates of return and do well for themselves and their clients. The remaining 80 percent—8 out of every 10 planners—aren't much more than a nice salesperson in a good-looking suit.

The unfortunate truth is that commission-based advisors can't always be counted on to give you advice that is in your best interest. They have too much incentive to sell you the investment products—life insurance, annuities, and mutual funds—that will earn them the highest commissions. If you aren't wealthy already, don't be naïve and think any planner is going to make you rich. Inform yourself. Understand the commission game. Before you ever buy an investment, ask to see the commission (plus bonus) disclosed in writing. Many people are stunned when they find out their planner frequently makes 80 percent to 85 percent commission (with bonus) or more of money invested in the first year.

I am not comfortable with recommending "traditional" financial planning to the average person because I know in my heart that it does not work. The planners available simply are not skilled in investing. They just regurgitate the sales pitch, sell on commission, and move on to the next client.

A list of the top 10 questions a novice investor is supposed to ask before working with a planner is just a sales pitch to get people to work with a planner who has certification, versus one who doesn't. It is not benevolent information to help the masses; it is designed to sell agents into getting a certificate, and to get people to go to those agents. To be blunt, if traditional financial planning even remotely worked, the financial education industry would barely exist.

So, who should use a planner and who shouldn't? If you are new to investing or less sophisticated and/or have an income that is at the middle-class earning range, then I recommend that you do not use a planner. You can buy the life insurance, mutual funds, and stocks you need online or over the phone and avoid most/all commissions. Let's be honest, you don't have many assets that need managing. Don't waste your money on fees and commissions. I am serious, there is *no reason* to pay commissions to someone who is not rich from investing themselves at this level. See my Chapter 7 and also investment authority Philip Springer's Chapters 16 and 17 for more information on picking good mutual funds and stocks.

But if your circumstances are different from the average person's, consider using a planner, but with these guidelines:

You have a reasonable amount of existing investment assets or capital, and/or earn well above-average income, and are committed to investing at least 10 percent of it. If your level of sophistication is low, then meeting with a planner can make sense, but follow these rules:

- No new planners. No planners in the bottom 80 percent in sales. Do *not* throw your money away.
- Ask to see their sales reports showing their rank in the office (they all have them). If the amounts of money are significant, ask to see how much they have invested in the investments they are recommending. Also ask to see a statement showing their investment returns for the previous year. Many will balk at those requests, and, if they do, then don't work with them.

- At this level, some will have a CFP or ChFC designation. This shows more commitment to education, which often (but not always) shows a better level of return for their clients.
- At this level, it can also make sense to go to a fee-only financial planner; planners who do not receive commission from their recommendations. You should only work with a fee-only planner if he or she will sign an agreement to act as a fiduciary for you. This is extremely important because some only want to be held to a "suitability" standard; meaning, they can recommend what is "suitable," rather than what they think is the best, and thus not look out for your interests. Those of you in the first bracket—sorry. You don't make enough money, or have enough money, to spend your money on a fee-only planner.

You are upper income and have substantial assets. Here a top planner makes sense for anything you don't do yourself.

- Seek out a top 5 percenter, or at the very least, a top 20 percenter. If fee-based, they charge much more than most fee-based planners. Make sure they are really at the top. Looks can be deceiving.
- Ask other wealthy people you know for referrals (Most top planners work on referral only, by the way, so you can't just walk in and say, "I want one.").
- Do your own due diligence. Look at their plan. Make sure it's more than picking a few stocks and life insurance. At this level, estate planning and asset protection are paramount. Again, I would need to see their investment results and personal earnings from investing, and have tremendous referrals as to their integrity and performance before turning over my money.

BUILD A TRUSTED TEAM

Be wary of well-intentioned friends and family members who want to guide you. I'm always amazed by the number of people with no real financial success who tell budding investors and entrepreneurs how they should conduct their business affairs. It's a strange phenomenon, but many people listen to naysayers who have never achieved financial success. Those who aren't financially successful whine and complain about missing out on investment opportunities after the fact, and they often try to discourage others from investing in smart investment vehicles.

Spend as little time and effort as possible discussing money or investments with these people. When they see you moving forward, their natural tendency is to criticize you, and try to convince you why you can't achieve your goals. Avoid discussing matters of finance with these people at all costs.

If your spouse or significant other happens to be one of these people, please don't argue with him or her. Let them be right in their own minds, for the time being—let your actions and results speak for you. As your family's situation improves financially, they will often begin to come around to a more positive way of thinking in regard to money. Here's a quick thought: Many spouses are resistant to investing. Maybe they have heard it all too many times already. However, they will come on board with getting debt-free. So, for faster momentum, get on board with the Burley debt-free program, and you just might see your spouse get on board with the rest.

Take advice from financially successful people who have proven themselves in the real world of investing. Contact them personally, if possible. Read their books, listen to their audio programs, and attend their seminars.

Do whatever is necessary to benefit from their financial expertise. If you need a real estate advisor, look at that person's investment portfolio. If he or she doesn't have a track record that supports his or her claims, continue your search. Not all are who they claim to be. If they are selling a "get-rich-quick" scheme, then keep your money.

I tried lots of the "get-rich-quick" stuff, and my money was gone—quick! Trust me on this. Trust only someone who has a long-term track record. Trust someone who tells you that success is achievable, but that it takes work. There is no "get-rich-quick" magic wand.

If you need legal advisors, find out how well they have defended and advanced the purposes of their clients. In other words, do some market research. When you assemble your team, base it on your level of sophistication, and where you want to go financially. If you are just starting out, you don't need Donald J. Trump's attorney. You have nothing he can help you with, and throwing away money for advice you can't use is as foolish as throwing it away on commissions without returns.

None of the advisors I work with were the first person I contacted. It took me a long time to find some of my advisors, while some were relatively easy to find. Please keep in mind the *5/15/80* rule. I tried several different people until I found those who actually knew what they were doing, and could perform by demonstrating a proven track record of consistently making their clients money. This is a process. You are looking for the top 20—if not the top 5—percent, so that means you will have some sorting and interviewing to do. The more you learn, the easier it is to discern whom to choose. Referrals from knowledgeable and wealthy people are especially valuable.

PLAYERS ON MY DREAM TEAM

I do work with the best professionals I can, and recommend you do the same, too. Make sure their knowledge/expertise matches your needs. The members on my team:

- *Financial planners:* As a planner myself, I don't need to retain this key advisor. Earlier in this chapter, we covered who should use a planner, and why. As discussed, for most people, deciding how to choose a planner is based on your emotions and level of experience. I'd like to offer some input on the thought processes of the two most extreme levels of investors:

1. For those with little experience, the tendency is to blindly trust a financial planner. This is very dangerous, because, as I explained earlier, 80 percent of all planners aren't successful, and they've been trained to lead clients toward products that generate the highest possible commissions, which inevitably leads to low returns. Most people who have planners do not get rich from their plan, or the advice given. Not even remotely. After commissions and fees, few people approach 10 percent returns, and many consistently lose money or make much less than 5 percent.

    If you hear yourself say, "I don't understand," let that be a warning sign. If a planner has sold you life insurance, mutual funds with high (over 3 percent) front-end loads, or "B" funds with no upfront commission (but as much as 20 percent in ongoing commissions), then do what Donald Trump would do, say: "You're Fired!" Even easier, don't tell them they are fired, simply cancel the products and replace them with ones that work for you, not their companies.

    It takes some very basic skills, and some action on your part. I am trying to help you, not make a commission. Fundamental financial planning is not that difficult.

    In the next chapter, we cover the basics of an Automatic Investment Plan and learn how to get out of debt and start replace saving with investing saving. You also cover your basic life insurance needs, if you have dependents. Most people need between

5 and 10 times their annual earnings. My advice here is, buy only term insurance. Term is basic coverage that pays when you die and has no investment. Any other type of investment insurance (whole life, universal life, adjustable life, variable life, etc.) is an extremely mediocre product because of the high commissions paid in the first year.

2. For those who consider themselves very experienced investors, yet often don't have consistent high-end investment results. I recommend that you take a good look at the reality of your beliefs. These investors often scoff at much of the advice I give, and believe they can outsmart the marketplace. Often, they earn a lot of money at their chosen career and think that makes them smarter and better investors. Yet they are among the worst investors in the world. Why? Their rates of return over the long run are usually poor because they believe, "You have to take *big risks* to make *big returns*." This simply is not true. Most investors get rich from investing small to medium amounts of money over the long term for an above average rate of return. On my web site, (johnburley.com), you will learn that the only way to truly make long-term high rates of return is to take low risk. That's right— high returns come from low risk, and low returns that come from high risk.

- *Attorney(s):* I own several businesses, and when I use an attorney, I use a specialist, not a generalist. I use several different types of attorneys:

1. Every few years, I have my *estate planning attorney* update my affairs. I don't recommend do-it-yourself kits in this area. If you're planning on being wealthy, and leaving an estate, pay a professional to set up an effective estate plan for you. (See Chapter 20 for more information on estate planning.)
2. To review contracts, several times a year, I consult with a *contract attorney*. Although I generally write my own contracts, I seek outside counsel to review the contracts.
3. I also work with several *real estate attorneys*. I use attorneys in several different geographic locations who specialize in evictions and foreclosures to protect my real estate income streams.

    When I need legal help, I pay for the best. I'm not a fan of paralegal services; they generally offer a very limited scope of services.

- *Accountant and bookkeeper:* My business volume warrants it, so we have a bookkeeper on staff who works very closely with the accountant. The accountant looks over the big picture and is involved in strategic planning. For my office, they are without question two of my most valued advisors. Based on your needs, I strongly recommend that you find people with strong backgrounds in tax and entity structuring who know how to use the right business structures for different types of business deals.

    Use common sense. If you own a business and don't have proper bookkeeping and accounting services, then you are being very foolish. Good bookkeeping and accounting is not an option; it's an absolute necessity. This function can often be outsourced, but I have a book-keeper on staff because we process hundreds of property payments per month, and work with several entities. I have an accountant because our tax returns are very detailed, and very complex, but she focuses on strategic planning. Some people picture their accountant as someone who rides over the hill with the bugle sounding to save the day, like the cavalry in old Western movies, but this is not what accountants do. Their job is not to save the day, but to count the bodies before the battle. Most accountants just count bodies; mine is a 5 percent one who actually does strategic planning, and they are rare. Understand the difference between standard accounting and tax return preparation (the counting of the bodies done after the battle); and strategic tax planning (done before the battle). Only a few accountants specialize in strategic planning, and one who can help lay out strategies to reduce the liability and manage cash flow can be a huge asset.

- *Insurance agent:* I have a very good and trusted insurance agent who handles the liability side of my insurance needs (property, auto, liability), which, in many cases, are required by law and/or the lender. We shop these aggressively to make sure the rates we are paying are competitive because rates can vary tremendously from company to company. For my own needs, I aggressively shop on the Internet for the lowest price available from only top-rated companies. This saves me thousands of dollars a year because I'm not dealing directly with a commission-driven sales agent.

    Life insurance is an absolute must for anyone who does not have the assets necessary to protect dependents. Only buy term insurance. Never buy investment life insurance (whole life, universal, variable, adjustable, etc.) unless you have very high-end estate planning issues. In which case, get a top 5 percent agent to handle that for you.

- *Brokers:* I work with several low, or no-commission, brokerages online to buy and sell stock and mutual fund investments, but in most cases, I make decisions on my own. From experience, few brokers can justify the fees charged, but if that fits your investment profile, then find a top one with confirmed results.
- *Real estate agent:* I am a professional real estate investor, so I work with quite a few real estate agents, in addition to having several agents on my staff. The top 20 percent are worth every dollar in commissions I pay. Again my advice is, hire a specialist. If you are renting out investment property, get an agent who does that. If listing your own home, get an agent who does that. And do *not* do business with the bottom 80 percent. The commission is the same, so get a top player to represent you.

These are the advisors I work with on an ongoing basis. Should the need arise for something not covered, I hire a specialist, not a generalist, and I advise you to do the same.

Some of your best financial advisors will be people you may never meet. I'm talking about reading their thoughts and ideas in books and articles, and attending events where they speak. Over the years, I have spent hundreds of thousands of dollars on books, audio and video programs, and seminars. In my office, I have an entire room that I converted into a library. The walls are filled from top to bottom with books, tapes, videos, CDs, and DVDs. The information I share with my readers and students is the essence of what I have learned from combining a quarter century of real world "street smarts" with expertise, study, and education.

One last word as we wrap up this chapter:

Being committed to building wealth is a continuous process, so jump in and start building your team!

For more information about searching for a Certified Financial Planner, visit the Certified Financial Planner Board of Standards (www.cfp.com). For fee-only planners, visit the web sites of the National Association of Personal Advisors (www.napfa.org) and the Garrett Planning Network (www.garret tplanningnetwork.com). For more information, visit johnburley.com/trump.

III

Act Now

7

ADOPT THE SEVEN
PRACTICES OF THE RICH
by
John R. Burley

Success leaves behind clues. Early in my adult life, I began to study the financial practices of remarkably wealthy people, paying close attention to their financial practices. If I could imitate their successful behaviors and follow their example in my own life, I reasoned, then I could discover my own path to financial freedom and wealth.

As I studied their money habits, I began to discover common threads woven throughout each of their stories. I took notes and began to develop a financial action plan. The good news—it worked! Today I am a wealthy investor because of what I discovered.

I named these clues, "Seven Practices of the Rich," and began to share them, first with my friends, and then with my students. If you are willing to study—and apply—these practices, then I believe that you, too, will be able to create a financial plan and build wealth:

1. Pay yourself first.
2. Reinvest your investment returns.

3. Receive automatic investor rates of return.
4. Pay attention to your money.
5. Adopt my automatic money system.
6. Become financially responsible.
7. Live debt-free.

My Seven Practices of the Rich are simple, and use common sense, but they are far from common. They may not be particularly glamorous, but their results are spectacular. Anyone who uses my Seven Practices can change their current financial position from uncertainty to security, and from scarcity to prosperity. Let's go into more detail, so that you fully understand their power.

PAY YOURSELF FIRST

The first practice of the wealthy is to pay yourself first. This does not mean going to the mall and buying a new shirt or television. That is not paying yourself; that is paying someone else. After all, how much real value do you actually receive from that shirt or television 10 or 20 years from now? Absolutely none!

Pay yourself first means that you invest your money so it grows for you, ideally through an Automatic Investment Plan (AIP). An AIP is any program where money is withdrawn, automatically and regularly from your paycheck or your checking or savings account, and invested on your behalf. Invest this money in a mutual fund, stock, or any other investment vehicle. Where you should place your AIP is based on your personal preference and investment expertise. We cover that topic in just a moment. The important thing right now is to understand the importance of starting and the cost of procrastination. Many people intend to start an AIP type investment program, but never do. Why do people put off such a huge, critical step to financial success? There are three primary "stories" people tell themselves that prevents them from becoming rich. These stories appear real, but they're simply not true. They are financial self-sabotage. Let me share them with you.

Story 1: A small amount of money put aside each month won't really make a difference. I need to get something bigger that will happen faster.

For most people, this never even vaguely occurs. Instead, they end up with nothing. Most rich people get rich on small amounts of money invested regularly at above-average rates of return. Here is a simple example to show just how easy it is to become a millionaire.

Assume a person earns $25,000 per year. They never get a raise and never get fired. They work from the age of 25 to 65. Over the course of their career, they will earn $1 million. If they take 10 percent ($2,500) of their annual income ($208 per month), and invest that money in a decent mutual fund, they will retire at 65 years old with $1 million ($2,500 $\times$ 9.08 percent = $1,000,000). So small amounts of money do matter. Someone making $25,000 a year can easily become a millionaire. Most people make way more than $25,000 per year but never become millionaires. So stop thinking investing small amounts of money won't help and start your AIP today.

Story 2: I can't afford it.

Every time I speak on this subject, I ask the audience if anyone has an AIP in place. Many raise their hands. I then ask them to stand up, and ask them to answer this simple question: Two months after you started your AIP, did you even notice that the money was gone from your monthly budget? The response is always an overwhelming "No." As you can see, "I can't afford it," is another self-sabotage story we buy. Most families see 20 percent to 40 percent of their money evaporate each month. Trust me on this. Start your AIP, and two months later you won't even notice that the money is gone. You will be on your path to becoming a millionaire.

Story 3: I need to research where to invest my money before I start.

This is "paralysis by analysis," and the third financial self-sabotage story. This is where you put off making any decision for fear of making a bad one. Don't fall for this trap. Take control and act. Start your AIP based on your level of investing expertise. You can always change your investment vehicle. The important thing is to start.

An AIP has these advantages:

- Easy to set up.
- Simple and hassle-free.
- Fun to watch as your money grows automatically.

Many experienced investors have an AIP linked to investment in the stock market; either to stocks directly or mutual funds. Unlike any other investment vehicle, the stock market has consistently produced compounded returns ranging from 10 percent to 12 percent, on average. Very few investments offer the benefits (appreciation and income) associated with ownership of stock over the long term. For the beginner, investing in the stock market offers the easiest way to invest for long-term growth. For further distinctions, read the next step.

Starting Your Automatic Investment Plan

There are two simple steps to starting your automatic investment plan:

1. Decide on your level of expertise.
2. Contact a broker or mutual fund company.

Most people will fall into one of five categories of investor "comfort," based on their experience and knowledge. Decide which of the following best suits you:

1. You want to invest in a mutual fund, but your budget doesn't provide the minimum entry and monthly contribution amounts required. Save the start-up amount in your bank account and commit to regular contribution amounts until you can activate and fund an AIP of your choice. To research performance and fees, you'll find resources in print (newspapers and investment magazines) and online about applying directly through fund brokers, and thus avoid brokerage fees. Sites such as morningstar.com, bloomberg.com, and others offer these services. If you can afford to buy this book, you can afford at least $100 a month to guarantee your financial future. No excuses! Take action now. Make your decision, and make that one phone call. There are companies that will let you start for as little as $50 per month if you invest in an IRA. American Century offers solid funds for this budget.

2. You want to invest wisely, but don't want to take the time to select individual stocks and investments, and prefer to have fund managers make investing decisions for you. I like Vanguard's Index 500 Fund, which has consistently outperformed over two-thirds of all managed funds over most annual periods in the past 40 years. For 10-year periods, the fund has outperformed more than 90 percent of the fund managers.

3. You are an experienced investor who wants to pick your own stocks and manage your monthly investment decisions, but with a broker's

help. Call your broker and request an AIP (direct debit/payroll deduction) form; if you don't already have a broker, you can start with the online brokerages listed in the next item.

4. You are a very experienced investor who can pick your own stocks and manage your monthly investment decisions without the help of a full-service broker. Use a fully automated online or discount broker to trade shares, access market information, and manage your portfolio. Watch for conditions and any hidden charges that may apply to transactions (i.e., some online brokers advertise low rates, but they are for market orders only, not the limit or stop orders that the most sophisticated investors use). E*Trade (etrade.com), Scottrade (scottrade.com), and TD Waterhouse (tdameritade.com) are a few of the discount brokers you can try online and by phone, and for frequent trades online. Keep abreast of new entrants in this market; larger banks now offer competitive rates and services. As rates, terms, and conditions change, you should continually research available brokers. Some also offer other services for a fee, such as news, research, charting, and analysis. Premium services are also usually available. Discount brokers are convenient, flexible, and, most importantly, charge low commissions. By the way, I receive no compensation, commission, or inducement of any description from any of the financial companies I reference in this chapter. My recommendations are based on my independent research of investment products and performances.

5. You already make a significant portion of your income from trading stocks or other investments. When trading for a living, avoid the two major pitfalls many business owners fall into: not paying themselves first and overpaying their taxes.

By separating a portion (10 percent) of your business income from your trading and diverting it into an AIP, you are consciously achieving the separation of business and personal investing that is vital to a sophisticated investor. This is a paramount form of protection. Things don't always work out as planned. And without the separation (psychologically, physically, and legally), you remain open to the risks of consumption and litigation with what is supposed to be your retirement money. I know a number of people who lost millions of dollars and had never separated their monies in this matter. The result: They were flat broke because, incredibly, they never set up an AIP, one of the simplest financial ideas. Even for the advanced investor, I cannot emphasize how important it is to separate your AIP money from your other money via an entity. If you are a successful investor, continue to do what you are doing—just put

10 percent of your money in a separate and distinct AIP account. Set up a separate entity (a limited liability corporation). Not only does this keep you on track psychologically and emotionally, but AIPs protect what you have created. The same would apply to other investment vehicles, such as real estate. Set up a separate and distinct AIP account. Then just continue to invest as usual.

Whatever you decide, do it today. An AIP is a critically important part of your financial action plan and a guaranteed way for you to pay yourself first, so that your money can begin working for you. Failure to set up an AIP is a disastrous financial mistake most people make. Most people don't have an AIP, and are poorer as a result—get the connection? Not doing an AIP produces less than nothing because the money you "coulda, woulda, shoulda" invested is gone and lost forever. If you fail to start your AIP, your rate of return is not zero, it's worse—minus 100 percent—because that money is gone forever. The choice not to do an AIP means you chose to lose 100 percent forever. Please make sure you don't make that decision. Instead make the decision to take power over your financial future by starting your AIP today. If it sounds like I'm repeating myself—I am. This is the most important step you can take, and yet most people don't do it.

Reinvest Your Investment Returns

Reinvesting is absolutely critical to your long-term financial success and the next important practice in your financial action plan. Many investors start out on the path to wealth by setting up an AIP. They watch their investment account grow, but then, it all comes to a grinding halt when they sabotage themselves by stealing earnings, cashing them out, and spending the returns. There is nothing wrong with enjoying the fruits of your labor, but if you truly want to create wealth, you must keep "hands off." Do this faithfully, and you will retire early and rich with very little effort. All you have to do is allow your money to fulfill its only purpose: to make more money. Don't steal from your financial future. Leave your money alone until it grows to where you can live off the income for the rest of your life. Following this step is really that simple.

Receive Automatic Investor Rates of Return

As an investor whose account grows automatically each month, your objective is to earn a minimum 10 percent to 12 percent return. I'm not talking about a year or two, but for the long term. This is actually much easier than it sounds, given the performance of the S&P 500 over time. Establish an AIP based on your level of investing expertise, but as your knowledge and experience grow, evaluate how to enhance your returns.

Also, be willing to spend some time actively managing your investment portfolio. How much time? About four hours a month. Give your investments some attention, and you'll be well on your way to building wealth. If you are more advanced, continue doing what you are already doing.

Pay Attention to Your Money

Many people have very little idea where all their money goes—all they know is that they don't have enough. When they look at their financial situation, they realize they should have more money left at the end of the month than they do. If you find yourself in this situation, try this experiment: For the next 30 days, write down everything you spend. I know that sounds like a lot of work, but it really isn't. Just jot down the figures, and add them up at the end of the month. This will impose a certain amount of accountability on your personal financial practices.

Think about it in bigger terms. Could a public company survive if it didn't account for 10 percent to 50 percent of its income each month? Yet, that's what most families lose every month because of careless expenditures. They just spend and spend, without knowing where their money goes. Most families don't follow this simple, but critical, step of tracking their money. Make sure that doesn't happen to you. Know exactly where your money goes.

Adopt My Automatic Money System

Following this practice is key to building wealth. I discovered that all wealthy people have some kind of money system they use. My Automatic Money System is a tool that helps you monitor and manage your financial goals. It's not a magic wand, or a slave driver's whip, and it's simple and flexible. Without one, you will have a very difficult time surviving financially.

What would happen if a public company didn't stick to any budget or system to monitor and manage income and expenditures? They'd go out of business, of course. Yet, that's where many families are headed, and that is tragic—and avoidable.

My money system is flexible enough to allow for any of life's surprises, but tight enough to warn you of potential problems before they get out of control. There are five steps, and in this order:

1. Automatic investment.
2. Debt elimination.
3. Charitable giving.
4. Debt avoidance strategies.
5. Life money.

In Chapters 8 and 9, I go into specific, step-by-step detail about my Automatic Money System and how it can work for you.

BECOME FINANCIALLY RESPONSIBLE

This practice is really quite simple to achieve. Use your common sense, and follow the Seven Practices of the Rich you learned in this chapter. Keep them at the forefront of your mind and use them in your day-to-day money decisions. You now have a financial advantage over most people: a simple process to follow to accumulate wealth and put your money to work for you. Ignoring this information, or pushing it aside, will rob you of the financial power you just gained.

LIVE DEBT-FREE

Living debt-free consists of sticking to two practices: never use consumer credit on the lender's terms, and always add 10 percent of your gross income to your minimum monthly debt payments. We'll talk about this practice in detail in Chapter 8, *Go on a Debt Diet*, but I want to stress that uncontrolled consumer credit can destroy your efforts to build wealth if you aren't careful.

You must learn to use consumer credit on your own terms, not those the lender imposes. How? Adopt a lifestyle that avoids debt. I'm not asking you to adopt a poverty-level lifestyle. I don't want you to lower your standard of living; in fact, I want you to increase your standard of living. As you do, you'll be able to own all the nice things you want, but you'll pay for them on a cash basis, not on a perpetual debt basis.

I trust that my Seven Practices have grounded you in establishing the successful money habits that can secure abundant wealth for you and family. These seven practices will ensure your financial success, so don't give me any more stories about why you can't save and invest. Take action and move forward on your path to financial freedom. For more information, visit johnburley. com/trump.

8

GO ON A DEBT DIET

by

John R. Burley

If your body is out of shape, you go on a diet. It's the same with fighting financial flab; to get out of debt, you go on a diet. It's a tough routine, learning how to lose fat and gain muscle, but once you get going, the process is exhilarating.

I learned to develop two new habits in fighting debt that I'd like to share with you. Integrate these principles in your new daily financial routine, and you'll get out of debt, too.

HABIT 1: NEVER USE CREDIT ON THE LENDER'S TERMS

Never use credit cards if you can't pay off the full balance every month. Ask yourself what's more important in your life—taking on more debt that weighs you down, or increasing the financial freedom that will help you reach your dreams?

If you're serious about becoming wealthy, but know you're not disciplined enough to use credit cards the smart way (paying off the balance in full every month), then cut up all of your cards and throw them away, except for a single no-fee credit card, tucked way down in the bottom drawer, for real emergencies.

Then pay cash for everything. I don't mean real cash—you'll miss out on all those airline frequent flyer points if you do. I rarely pay with actual cash; instead, I use the modern-day equivalent: an American Express card that I pay off in full each month, along with a no-fee Visa card, if a merchant doesn't accept American Express. I always pay off my Visa card in full each month, too. As an added plus, both cards give me an itemized record of my spending, which is useful in tracking my expenses for tax purposes.

What I'm saying is—and I can't stress this enough—I treat my credit cards as a convenient way of spending cash, not as a source of credit for spending cash I don't have.

If you're deeply in debt, but unwilling to destroy your credit cards, then I'm sorry to say that you are headed one way toward a financial train wreck.

End the cycle now. Gather all your credit cards, and lay them out in front of you. They are tantalizing, but ignore their glossy sheen. Think instead about all the problems they have caused you: the growing debt, the endless monthly payments, the debt bondage.

Cut them up. I mean it. Stop reading and cut those cards up *now*. Get out a pair of scissors and take the first step toward living a debt-free life. Pay careful attention here. If you are constantly carrying credit card debt and have not cut up your cards, you're standing on shaky ground. For this information to help you, you must be willing to help yourself.

If you can't take this step, I urge you to get help. Contact one of the many nonprofit, credit counseling agencies that are available to you, either on a walk-in basis or over the phone. Check the Internet or your local phone book for debt consolidation and credit counseling agencies. When choosing, make sure you work with a nonprofit group. The credit counseling industry has deservedly earned a bad reputation over the past few years. Some agencies hide behind their nonprofit status, but they are actually fronts for credit card companies and nothing more than debt collection services. Others charge large fees and offer you little that you could not do on your own. Unfortunately, there is no national company I can wholeheartedly recommend, but there may be private agencies to contact.

If you regularly attend a church, synagogue, mosque, or other religious service, your pastor or leader may be aware of agencies or ministries that offer debt counseling. Take advantage of these resources. Don't think that you have to face this battle on your own. There really are people who can help you. Debt can be negotiated down, interest lowered, and, in some cases, removed, but keep in mind that you still must repay much of what is owed because of the new bankruptcy legislation.

If, and only if, you are determined to discipline yourself in using credit cards from now on, consider canceling your old card(s) and transferring the balance to new cards that offer a low "honeymoon," or zero-interest introductory rate for the first year. You may be able to cut your interest payments substantially, which means you can direct more money to paying off the balance sooner. Make sure that you ask and confirm, in writing, that any balance transfers aren't counted as cash advances by the new lender, so interest accrues at a much higher rate.

Then, after doing your research on available rates, play the credit card game. Contact online sources such as bankrate.com, cardratings.com, and cardweb.com to compare card offers. Call your current company and ask them to match your new offer, or say that you'll switch. If you do switch, eliminate the old ones first. Transfer balances, destroy old cards, and cancel the account in writing. Don't order new cards until you do; if you don't take this step, you'll simply have more cards to get you into more trouble, and more debt.

Transferring balances reduces the amount of interest paid and accelerates the elimination of your debt. Do not fall for the ploy of refinancing old debt for new debt by accepting lower payments and a longer payoff. Keep your payments level. That way, more will go to principal and decrease the time to pay off the debt.

The same applies for rolling debt into a home refinance or second mortgage. This is a huge trap created by lenders, not to provide you with relief, but to make them rich. Don't play their game, which is to transfer the balance and only pay the lower minimum payment during the teaser period—and then be right back where you were in six months to a year when the rate ratchets up. The smart thing to do is to use the lower interest rate as an opportunity to terminate as much of the balance as possible.

HABIT 2: ESTABLISH YOUR DEBT ELIMINATION PLAN

The second key to escaping from the trap of debt is to establish a good debt elimination plan. We mentioned these plans in Chapter 5. Here's how these plans work: You commit 10 percent of your gross income to your minimum monthly credit card payments. If your gross income is currently $3,000 a month, and your minimum monthly payments are $1,200, you now start paying $1,500 a month toward your debt. Don't add that 10 percent to each of your debts—put *all* of that money on the debt you can eliminate the fastest.

That will help you build momentum and see results more quickly, which will give you the boost you need to keep going. Plan on committing 10 percent of your gross income to this task. That may be too much for some of you, but start with as much as you can. The point is to start. Now!

Now let's walk through five steps to financial freedom, step by step:

1. *Organize your debts.* Organize all your debts in one pile, including credit and charge cards, loans, mortgages, and any other debt.
2. *Take inventory.* Make a list of all your debts on a separate piece of paper. You'll need this information to calculate your debt elimination plan on the worksheet that follows (Exhibit 8.1). List the name of the debt, the total payoff balance, and the monthly payment. You'll need this information for the next step. Before we move on, let me add a word of encouragement: Viewing your total debt can be depressing, but don't be discouraged—you're doing something about your debt today. You're establishing a plan to get rid of your debt—forever. You're taking control of your financial future—right now.
3. *Determine your pay-off ratio and pay-off priority.* Now you need to figure out which debt to pay off first, which is part of building a workable

Downloadable Exhibit 8.1   Debt Elimination Plan*

Line One: _____
Debt Name (List to whom you owe the money):

Line Two: _____
Total Balance (Fill in the current total balance owed):

Line Three: _____
Monthly Payment (Fill in your current minimum monthly payment):

Line Four: _____
Pay-Off Ratio. Divide the current total balance owed (Line Two) by the minimum monthly payment (Line Three), and enter your answer on Line Four. This is your payment-to-debt ratio for each debt.

Line Five: _____
Pay-Off Priority. Start with the lowest ratio number from Line Four in deciding which bill to pay off first. The lower the ratio number, the higher the pay-off priority. Number each one of your debts.

Source: Copyright: johnburley.com. For any other use, contact John Burley at johnburley.com.
*Note: A blank version of this exhibit can be downloaded from www.trumpuniversity.com/wealthbuilding101 for your personal use.

strategy. Without a step-by-step process, chances are your debt won't budge. I recommend that you pay off your debt based on what I call a pay-off ratio score, which I'll explain in the next step.

Follow the easy steps described in Exhibit 8.1: Debt Elimination Plan.

4. *Pay off your debt.* Start with the debt that has the highest pay-off priority number. Put 10 percent of your gross income on this one debt and make a new, higher payment. At the same time, you must take two other actions simultaneously: Continue making the monthly minimum payments required on all other debts; and refrain from creating any additional debt. Pay off all debts in this way until you are completely debt-free (including the debt on your house and cars).

5. *Invest your debt money.* Once you have completed the process of paying off all your debt, invest the money you once used to pay to service debt to invest instead. That's right. Since the money was already gone (or spent), you really won't miss it. So now put that money to work for you. This step is critical to forging a new path on your journey to financial freedom. Instead of spending it, use the money you just released from servicing your debt to building your financial freedom.

By rolling the additional 10 percent of your gross income, plus each and every minimum monthly payment to the next debt, you then have all of that money to invest. This will make you richer faster than you ever imagined. You will pay off all your debt and not take on new debt to replace it. Keep rolling the money from one debt to the next, terminating each as you go. In this way, you build momentum until you are totally debt-free.

Instead of just spending the money, you now use that money to build a better financial future for yourself and the people you love. Do not—I repeat, do not—fall back into the same old debt cycle by servicing new (noninvestment) debts. Put this money to work for you. My program, "How to Become Totally Debt-Free (Including Your House and Cars) in 3–7 Years!" is available as a free download at johnburley.com/trump. You will receive the downloadable worksheet, the calculator to determine which debt to pay off first, and be able to calculate your financial freedom date.

A DEBT ELIMINATION STORY: STAN AND BARBARA

Let's look at how a couple named Stan and Barbara succeeded in becoming debt-free. Their story is a great example of the power you, too, can achieve.

Exhibit 8.2   Stan and Barbara's Debt

Type of Debt	Balance ($)	Monthly Payment ($)
Consumer debts	14,600	790
Car loans	15,000	565
Mortgages	120,000	1,320
Total	149,600	2,675 min.

Debt termination money of extra 10% = $268 per month

This 40-year-old married couple with two young children earned a comfortable annual income of almost $70,000, yet they were deeply in debt and struggling to pay their bills each month (Exhibit 8.2). Worse, they had no plan for how they were going to pay for their children's educations and fund their own retirement. I was working as a financial planner when they contacted me. They were frantic. Every one of the many advisors they had consulted said that their best solution was to file for bankruptcy.

Like so many other consumers, they were giving away a large part of their income to bill collectors every month. They were carrying $14,600 in consumer debt, and paying approximately $790 in minimum monthly payments. In addition, they owed $15,000 on two cars, and $120,000 on two mortgages, with monthly payments of $565, and $1,320, respectively. Talk about sticker shock. Their total monthly debt payments added up to $2,675.

Stan and Barbara's financial situation was really bleak. They were buried in debt and broke. They didn't have any savings for emergencies, and their spending was so far out of control that they were buying groceries on their credit cards. If a real emergency hit them, they'd be in serious trouble. Those "easy" monthly payments had boxed them into a corner, so that $2,675 in payments really wasn't theirs.

Worse, that $2,675 is gone forever every month because they haven't learned to properly manage their habit of uncontrolled consumption. Listen closely because this is the really dangerous part of the debt trap: Most people in this trap continue to buy new stuff, even before they pay off the old stuff. With this program, we will pay off all the debts and not take on new debt to replace the old debt. We will keep rolling the money forward from one debt to another, terminating each debt (one after another) forever, and building more and more momentum until you are totally debt-free. Then—and this is the exciting part—we will roll all that money forward into an AIP to ensure continuing financial freedom.

Once I understood how Stan and Barbara spent their money, I showed them how my plan could work for them. They were able to take control of their spending. Then they committed to start reducing their expenses and also agreed to commit to adding 10 percent of their minimum monthly payments ($268) to their debt elimination plan. The important thing is to make a sincere start.

Stan and Barbara took the original debt payment ($2,675), added 10 percent ($268), and put that total ($2,943) into an AIP. By doing that, Stan and Barbara can pay off all their debt and be on their way to becoming multimillionaires. In little more than five years, when all their debt is paid off, that money gets redirected into an AIP. By the time they are ready to retire, this supercharged AIP will grow to several million dollars.

It's that simple. It really works. This is a powerful system. My program has worked for Stan and Barbara, thousands of my students, and it can work for you, too. Follow the steps and you, too, will be debt-free and rich faster than you ever imagined.

Stan and Barbara's New Financial Future

By following my debt elimination plan (DEP), this family will be completely debt-free, including their house and cars, in about five years. At 65, by investing the recaptured debt money into an automatic investing program, they will be millionaires.

How will they do it? They start with one car payment, which costs $300 a month, and add the entire amount they currently can afford ($268) to this bill. By paying $568 every month, they'll be able to wipe out the balance on their second car in less than six months.

Now they take that money, $568, and apply it to their next highest priority debt. It's critical to understand that you apply all of that 10 percent until you are debt-free. For me, before I resolved to change, after paying off a car, I would just spend that $300 a month car payment on something else; now, under my debt elimination plan, you don't buy something else and continue the debt cycle. You keep strategically applying that money to other debts until *all* of your debt is paid off.

Stan and Barbara's next priority is their Visa debt. The power of this plan is really exciting as you watch: They take the entire $568 and add it to Visa's monthly payment of $300 a month. The $868 they now have to wipe out their Visa debt will wipe out their $3,600 balance in about four months. By using my plan, they can pay off their second car and their Visa bill in 10 months, instead of years.

Next they'll turn their attention to a department store charge account ($675), which they wipe out in one month. There's a surplus left over ($263), so they apply that toward their bank Visa card debt. I think you get the idea. We go from one debt to another until all debts are paid off. In 21 months, they pay off all of their consumer debt and automobile loan, and then turn the full force of their money to paying off their house four years later.

Add up the new figures, which are pretty impressive: This family, which was in debt up to their eyeballs, is completely debt-free in five and a half years. But the best is yet to come. Stan and Barbara now have $2,943 per month to invest (the $2,675 original total of minimum payments, plus the $268 debt termination money).

They now have in their hands the money they previously gave away to lenders every month, but instead of spending it and buying more stuff—they invest it. Please remember for all intents and purposes, this money was gone. It was no longer theirs. They were giving it away. They did not have access to it. It was not theirs. What they have done is powerfully take it back, and now use it to make them secure. By investing that $2,943 every month for the next 20 years in an AIP fund (we will assume a return of 10 percent here), their money will grow to $2.2 million by the time they reach 65. Stan and Barbara not only get out of debt—they become millionaires.

Imagine that. Isn't it amazing how simple becoming rich really is?

Your Debt-Free Date

To determine how long it will take you to become completely debt-free, add up your debt, and calculate your payoff. Ideally, this should be 10 percent of your gross income. If you can't set this aside, put down what you can, but start somewhere. Then determine how many years it will take for you to become completely debt-free. Using this strategy, most families can become completely debt-free, including their home and cars, in three to seven years. My debt elimination plan is simple and realistic. It has worked for thousands of people, and I know it can work for you.

Some key thoughts: Right now, don't worry about which account has the highest interest rate. This plan accelerates your debts so quickly that the few months you pay higher interest won't make that much of a difference. Most of you will be able to stick to the process described, and pay off your debt. For many of you, I know that it is not possible to reduce the rates you are paying, but if you can reduce the interest rate you are paying as described earlier, do so. Then simply recalculate the pay-off ratio to determine the new pay-off priority. Adjust as required.

The key to this process is momentum; as you see bills completely eliminated, it becomes much easier to keep going. You gain enthusiasm and a real sense of achievement.

In many cases, if you currently have a lot of debt, you won't qualify for lower interest rates, so, if you can, apply for them now and transfer your higher interest balances, or refinance all of your smaller consumer debts with a low-interest personal loan.

Remember, your goal is not to establish more credit, but to lower, and eliminate, the interest you pay. If you do get new lower-rate cards, remember what I said earlier. Cancel your old cards and cut them up once the balances are paid off, so you don't leave yourself open to future temptation. Consumers become deeply in debt for one reason: a lack of control. The last thing you want is a pile of cards that tempt you to get back into the spending game. I can tell you, the consequences will very likely be much worse the second time around.

One last warning: If you refinance or lower the interest rate on existing debt, don't fall into the trap of making the new lower payment. Consumers often do this. It's grasping at straws, and it spells disaster. You can take out a new loan with a lower interest rate, and often a longer term, which does lower your monthly payments—but pushes you right back into the lender's trap. Guaranteed, you'll be in debt longer, pay more in interest, and be tempted to consume more new debt to absorb the "extra" monthly money you now have to spend. The reason you got a new loan was to pay off your debt—not add to it.

This isn't the only debt reduction plan available. It is, however, super simple, easy to use, and works fast. If you get bogged down in the details, just remember these simple principles:

- Get rid of unnecessary credit cards immediately. Most of us only need one or two credit cards for emergencies. For nonemergencies, I recommend a card such as American Express or a debit card that requires you to pay the outstanding balance in full each month.
- Pay only cash (or the modern equivalent; a card that requires you to pay off the balance in full every month), and avoid charging unnecessary consumer items again.
- Start and stick to the debt elimination plan.
- Schedule a date in three to seven years to become debt-free.
- Remember to focus on the end result of financial freedom when you are tempted to slip back into old habits.

Without the burden of debt, all of us would be happier and healthier, financially and otherwise, and the world would be a better place, too. Everyone can live debt-free.

Start spreading the news! For more information, visit johnburley.com/trump.

9

IMPLEMENT AN *I DON'T WANT TO DO A BUDGET* AUTOMATIC MONEY SYSTEM

by
John R. Burley

It's a fact of life, especially financial life. Everyone needs to budget.

Many people—including me—don't like hearing that they have to limit their spending. They don't even like hearing the word budget.

Here are some of the objections I hear whenever the word budget enters a conversation:

- Budgets are too restrictive and limiting. They take away my freedom.
- Budgets are too complicated. They're hard to follow.
- Budgets really don't work. They set you up for failure.
- Budgets aren't fair. They cause arguments.
- Budgets make me feel bad. I don't want to know what a poor manager I am.

The list goes on and on. You can undoubtedly add your own objections.

That's why I prefer to talk about budgets in a different way. A budget makes you work for your money. Instead, I talk about a "money system" that makes your money work for you, which is essentially what we want our budgets to accomplish.

For the average family to understand and more importantly use, a budget has to be simple. Many families set up budgets to control their expenses, but these budgets rarely work over the long term. Budgets also create a lot of stress among family members. Sometimes, they destroy the family's finances, and often relationships, because of the fighting that erupts over money. That's the short history of budgets and, unfortunately, despite their good intentions, for most families, budgets only bring failure.

Simply stated, a budget should be just a tool that helps you monitor, achieve, and maintain your financial goals. A budget, or money system, should serve you—not master you. The operative word here is "should."

For many years, I disliked budgets so much I tried to find ways not to do one. If I could find just one example of a successful company that didn't follow a budget, then I promised myself I wouldn't, either.

Well, guess what? After several years, it became obvious to me that there wasn't one successful company or operation that didn't have the financial controls in place to be successful.

Those were the cold hard facts, whether I liked them or not: To obtain long-term financial freedom, I had to develop and implement a system for managing my money, too. For me to follow a budget faithfully, and ultimately, successfully, it had to be different. This new system had to be the mirror opposite of the old system. It had to:

- Be easy and fun to follow.
- Not take up a lot of time.
- Provide freedom for fun consumption.
- Be simple and not require me to have to watch every penny all of the time.
- Give immediate results.
- Have no more than a handful of steps (say, five).
- Produce a chunk of money for investment that could eventually provide enough cash flow to live on for the rest of my life.
- Pay off all my consumer debt within a reasonable period of time.
- Allow me to donate money to my favorite charities.
- Provide true long-term financial freedom.
- Be automatic and so easy I could forget about it after setting it up.

In summary, I needed an easy-to-follow money system that would allow me to actually *budget* for my personal financial growth. I called my new system: My "I Don't Want to Do a Budget!" Automatic Money System.

Automatic Money System

When I introduce my automatic money system (AMS) to the students who attend my seminars, I start by asking them how they feel about budgets. After the groans and complaints subside, I tell them I agree with them; in fact, when it comes to budgets, I'm the "anti-financial planner." I say, "Budgets suck!" Then I give them permission to tell everyone they know that a financial authority said so, and tell them to feel free to list all the reasons why that's true.

Then they all stand up and, fists punching the air, yell out a few resounding choruses of "Budgets suck!" Silly as it sounds, this fun exercise is useful: it helps purge the old psychological notions of what a budget means to your lifestyle. It helps clear out the negative expectations and experiences of how much work budgets are and how complicated a traditional budget can be to implement and follow.

Right now, you can get rid of those same negative thoughts, too. On the count of three, stand up, pump your fist in the air, and let out a loud cheer: "Budgets Suck!"

One . . . Two . . . Three . . . budgets suck! Right! Feel better? Good.

Now let's get ready to adopt a new mindset. My system is all about fun and freedom because it follows one simple principle: Put as much emphasis on the plus side of the equation (income, savings, and investing), as you do on the negative (or expense) side of the equation (which is the only side traditional budgets emphasize, by the way). By achieving that balance, you "budget" for your personal financial growth and build the wealth that you truly desire to possess. This is your system, so have fun with it. There's no need to sacrifice all the things you want; in fact, this system works because you leave yourself some room for fun.

There are five simple, powerful steps that lead you to your financial freedom so you can build wealth. Let's look at and briefly discuss each of them in turn.

1. *Implement an automatic investment plan.* As described in Chapters 7 and 8, you must set up an automatic investment plan (AIP) and contribute at least 10 percent of your gross income every month to

systematically build wealth. Then invest this money in your AIP at your level of investment expertise. This will immediately begin to put your money to work for you. Ten percent might sound like a lot, but it isn't. If you can't set this much aside, then begin with less. But the point is—begin! My students tell me they don't even notice that missing 10 percent. This is the first step in your new money system. Remember the three stories that sabotage this step: "small amounts of money don't matter," "I can't afford it," and "I don't know where to put the money." Any of these excuses guarantee you a rate of return of minus 100 percent because the money is gone—spent—never to be seen by you again. Stop the madness. If you haven't already done so, start your AIP now.

2. *Adopt a debt termination plan.* As spelled out in our discussion about debt termination in Chapter 8, contribute another 10 percent of your gross income and systematically reduce your debt every month. By doing this faithfully, you will be completely debt-free in three to seven years, including your house and car(s).

3. *Institute a charitable giving plan.* Contribute at least 10 percent of your gross income to charity. It's part of the responsibility and reciprocity associated with creating and being a good steward of wealth. All wealthy people I know give to charity. It also keeps them balanced and puts them in the mindset of generosity which allows them to receive as well as give.

Most ancient sacred texts discuss giving to others, and for this reason alone, giving should be seen to be incredibly important. It is clear in life that we get in proportion to what we give. The physical and psychological act of regularly giving turns on the opportunity for you to make and receive more and more. Interestingly, most poor to middle-class people don't regularly give to charity, while the vast majority of rich people do. Success leaves behind clues, so here is my thought for you on contributing:

If you don't give and you are not rich (and almost all rich people give), what do you have to lose by trying? Nothing! It works. Do it!

I strongly suggest that you institute a charitable giving plan as part of your new money system. Some of you may be thinking: "I can't figure out how I'm going to squeeze out 10 percent for investing, and you want me to commit another 10 percent for debt, and another 10 percent for charity? There's no way I can do this. I just can't afford it."

I understand. I've been there. My advice is to start, and start *now*. If you can commit only a few percent in each of these critical areas, that's okay. You can increase the percent bit by bit every month, until you reach the full 10 percent in each of these three critical areas. The key is to start now. These actions will give you the momentum to keep moving forward and become financially free.

4. *Live a debt-free lifestyle*. Getting out of debt means not creating more debt in its place—that is just common sense. Part of your new money system must include this new lifestyle. Simple strategies can help, such as paying only cash (which includes credit cards that you must pay off in full each month), and maintaining control on their use. I look at it this way: Many people say, "I want a new suit." If you can't pay for the suit in full when the bill comes, then you don't need a new suit! Only buy what you can afford. Live within your means for a short time and you will be able to live in a manner you never thought possible for the rest of your life.

5. *Spend the rest (party!)*. Here's the easy part. After faithfully implementing these strategies, and paying your basic bills—spend the rest of your money. Yes, that's what I said. Spend it—guilt free and as much as you want. What most people find is now they buy what they really want, rather than a bunch of stuff. So, in the end, they have better stuff and a lot more money. Why don't you do it? Start now. That's part of the beauty of this simple system. It gives you the flexibility to spend all the rest of your money on whatever you want.

By now I trust you can begin to see that this five-step "budget" isn't a budget that makes you work hard—but an automatic system that works hard for you.

For most people, this system will be very simple and painless to implement. For those who are currently very overextended and/or living way beyond their means, this is a money system they will need to ease into gradually. Regardless of your income and your current level of expenses, you can succeed with this system. For some, it will require some minor adjustments; for others, it may demand serious adjustments to lifestyle, on either the income or expenditure side, or both, before it will properly function. Some people are living the lifestyle they want now, but can't afford; once they implement my new money system, they'll be able to afford the life they want to live.

This system works. I have thousands of students throughout the world who have achieved the carefree existence of semi-retirement by following these five simple steps.

If, however, you are among those people who require serious changes to make my automatic money system work, don't be discouraged. By deciding to start, you are heading in to the right direction. Keep going! It is ultimately your choice. I sincerely trust you decide to accept the short-term pain of change rather than endure the long-term pain of financial ruin.

Now let's turn our attention to a few strategies that make this new money system work in the easiest way possible.

Reduce Your Expenses

For the average family, it is often easier to reduce expenses than to increase income. The objective here is to simplify your life, not make it more complicated. Comb through your expenses. While looking through the old receipts, notice how many purchases gave you little, or any, pleasure. Many people also find they are paying for services they don't really need.

Here are a few fast and easy ways to reduce expenses:

1. When you go shopping, leave your wallet at home. Browse before you buy, and come back later; you'll end up buying less.
2. Be aware of marketing techniques to get you to buy more. Take your name off catalogue mailing lists, telephone lists, and e-mail lists.
3. Don't buy from solicitors or donate to charities over the phone.
4. Get rid of ATM cards.
5. Never use "pay day" lenders.
6. Keep a written record of all expenses for 30 days.
7. Never pay full retail for anything.
8. Always ask for discounts, use two-for-one coupons, buy online, and buy from classified ads.
9. Spend half as much on Christmas presents.
10. Buy small business items at discount shops rather than at office supply stores.
11. Investigate phone carriers for calling interstate and overseas. Be aware of when you use your cell phone, and the rates involved.
12. Research travel costs. Use Internet sites that offer advertised or "low-bid" specials, or travel stand-by.
13. Borrow books from the library instead of buying them, and sell your used books.
14. Do your grocery shopping once a week instead of impulsively and unplanned. Use a prepared list. Buy generic and in-house brand grocery lines if quality is the same.

15. Buy clothing at the end of the season for discounts.
16. Make your next car a new used car. Maintain and service your car to reduce breakdowns. Shop automobile insurance online to make sure you are getting the best rates.
17. If eligible, obtain discount rates for seniors.

As you take the time to track your expenses, you will most likely notice a trend: the tendency to spend money without thinking where your dollars go. Look at your unconscious spending and knock out purchases that are unnecessary. This simple practice can free up your money—and make more of it available for investing, eliminating debt, and contributing to charity. You may be very surprised by how much money you pay in interest charges ever year. Just think how different your financial statements will look when none of your money is spent on interest.

Computerize

If you are reasonably computer literate, I highly recommend that you use one of the many personal finance programs available. My family and I have used Intuit's Quicken and Microsoft Money. Such programs allow you to budget, itemize your expenses, store all your income tax information, track your investments, do online banking, and much more. Personally, I find Quicken to be very powerful and user friendly. You can find this program, and others, at most office supply or electronics stores.

Watch for Red Flags

These red flags are:

- Expect to make some mistakes during the process.
- Be prepared to be flexible. Plan for some unexpected expenses.
- Double check your entries to make sure you don't overlook quarterly, semiannual, or annual expenses.
- Always expect the unexpected, especially in the beginning.

Be consistent and keep the family involved at all crucial times. The biggest budget problems usually result from lack of family involvement. Many times I have seen one of the parents take off like the Lone Ranger and attempt to manage everything on his or her own. This usually involves one person setting up the new financial program and then inflicting the finished product on the rest of the family. Often this is followed by a lecture, finger-pointing, yelling, fighting, and screaming.

Don't do this! Don't start your new financial system on your own or in a confrontational way. Work as a team. Involve the entire family from the beginning. There are two good reasons to do this: First, you need their help. With everybody involved, you greatly reduce the potential of overlooking certain expenses or income sources. Second, if anyone is left out of the planning process, they may resent the sudden imposition of new spending rules and not cooperate.

Avoid Impulse Buying and Spending

Think about how you spend your money. Buy only what you truly want. A little instant gratification won't kill you, but a lot surely will. Where needed, strive to impose more control on your spending.

Over the course of a month, keep a detailed record of how you spend your money. Write down every expenditure so that you can observe your financial habits and your family's. Doing this will allow you to see where you really are financially and help you commit to using the automatic money system. Remember, you don't work for this new money system—it works for you. Stick with it, and you'll reap the rewards. For more information, visit johnburley.com/trump.

IV

BE THE BOSS: THE ENTREPRENEUR'S PATH TO WEALTH

10

THINK LIKE AN ENTREPRENEUR
by
Michael E. Gordon, PhD

I know from personal experience that entrepreneurship is a tool that can create great wealth and personal enrichment in your life. Six of my 11 start-up companies were successes, and one was sold to a public British company. The five nonsuccesses (the word failure is not in my vocabulary), while they never generated revenue, did not weaken me at all. In fact, they enriched my chances of future success immeasurably because of what I learned and applied.

This chapter clarifies any misconceptions you may have about your ability to succeed in your own business by explaining the 11 essential entrepreneurial power skills that you can learn and develop.

ENTREPRENEURIAL MISCONCEPTIONS

The entrepreneurship literature is full of paralyzing drivel about the failure rates of new start-ups, the massive sacrifices entrepreneurs must make, the loss of job security, the financial risks, the long hours, the stress and frustration, and so on and so on. I have two words for all of this:

Bull Cookies!

Look around you and imagine the vast wealth in businesses. *Every business, from the largest to the smallest, resulted from entrepreneurship.* According to BizStats. com, there are 24 million businesses in the United States, of which 18 million are sole proprietorships—owned and operated by one individual. Many small business owners are also part- and full-time employees while they maintain their day jobs. According to the U.S. Census Bureau, in 2003 alone (most recent figures available), almost three quarters of a million Americans started their own businesses.

I never feel more alive than when I am on the entrepreneurial trail. There is no job where I could ever have made the kind of money I have made as my own boss. Stress and frustration? The worst career stress and frustration I ever experienced was working for someone else, accepting a nominal salary, putting up with corporate political nonsense, and lacking the personal freedom to pursue my own innovative, value-creating ideas.

The fact is, if you take it thoughtfully, and step by step, your chances of success are excellent. You need less talent, skill, industry knowledge, money, and other resources than you may believe. You can outsource most functions— design, manufacturing and packaging, marketing and sales, distribution, shipping, and accounting. The resources you can mobilize on the Web are nearly limitless. And, if you control your financial exposure and don't make it on the first attempt, you'll be better prepared for your next start-up.

Dictionaries define entrepreneurship as the start-up, growth, and management of a business, for profit, with great initiative and the assumption of risk. I see it more creatively and personally: Entrepreneurship encompasses mind set, action, and process (MAP) guiding you to the wealth you want.

Mindset: Entrepreneurs go through the world continuously seeking ideas and opportunities to commercialize. They focus on innovating, doing things better, adding, creating, and *delivering* unique value to customers and to all stakeholders. And they want to be rewarded for their successes. The more value they add, the greater their financial rewards.

Actions: Entrepreneurs are proactive to the extreme, and once on the opportunity trail, they move mountains to mobilize the necessary resources to accomplish their goals. Following the Nike motto, they *just do it!* and they do it their own way.

Process: Entrepreneurship is a dynamic, continuous, living process. You, the entrepreneur, founder, and champion, drive the process, from the idea through wealth creation. Along the path, you will mobilize resources, build your team, devise an astute strategy, develop your business plan, capture that first magic customer, and manage the challenges of growth—the ultimate in personal enrichment.

There are four compelling reasons to start your own business.

You Realize Your Personal Potential

Before I became an entrepreneur, I worked as a chemical engineer for 10 years. Although I had an excellent job at a prestigious company, a gnawing entrepreneurial desire grabbed hold of me and wouldn't let go. Together with a friend and coworker, we began looking around for ideas and opportunities, and latched onto one that looked particularly attractive. We put together a simple business plan and began pursuing our start-up in the evenings and on the weekends while we kept our day jobs. My growing family, a mortgage, limited borrowing power, and nail-biting uncertainty caused me to be risk averse, but I refused to let these obstacles cloud my vision. Before our start-up had any revenues, the rewards from pursuing my dreams went sky high. I felt energized, self-reliant, unstoppable! I was experiencing these entrepreneurial benefits:

- The possibilities of creating unique value from practically nothing.
- The courage and the passion to "go for it;" to achieve my life goal.
- The satisfaction of becoming my own boss and being rewarded for my hard work.
- The pride of developing my personal entrepreneurial power.
- The warm glow of self-confidence and self-esteem *just from trying*.
- The satisfaction of being in control of my most precious asset—my time.
- The excitement of visualizing the unimaginable financial doors that were about to open for me and my family.

You Reap—and Keep—a Lot of Money

The business was able to generate some sales and profits while I was still working at my day job. Then, when the risks seemed minimal and the potential looked wide open, I left my day job to grow the business full time.

Although personal potential is an enticing reason to become an entrepreneur, the real payoff is financial in these four ways:

1. The income stream from the profitable sales of your products and services.
2. The harvest of your business, either by taking your business public, selling it to a motivated acquirer, or continuing to reap the rewards of growth.
3. Tax deductions for legitimate expenditures in pursuit of business activities.
4. Asset and personal liability protection.

The first two points are self-evident; only the last two need more explanation. Attorney and tax strategist J.J. Childers addresses these topics in more detail in Chapter 18, "Save Money with These Tax Strategies," and Chapter 20, "Protect Your Assets."

Tax Deductions

You can deduct taxes for legitimate start-up and operating business expenses, including:

- Personal or corporate vehicles for business-related activities.
- Business-related travel expenses (marketing, sales, and customer relations; sourcing of products and training distributors; attending trade shows and sleuthing competitors; and the like).
- Entertainment expenses directly related to doing business.
- Medical and dental benefits, and pension and profit sharing, if your corporation funds such plans.
- Benefits to hire and pay family members.
- Continuing education to maintain and increase your skills.
- Charitable contributions.

Carefully document all expenses, and keep accurate records and time logs.

Asset and Personal Liability Protection

Keeping the money you earned through entrepreneurship requires that you attend to the issues of asset and personal liability protection. You and your family are vulnerable and can be attacked by lawsuits for a wide variety of reasons. Don't underestimate this risk. If, however, you set up the appropriate corporate structure or limited partnership for your business, *and maintain it properly*, you can minimize your personal liability. Several legal vehicles accomplish this protection: the C corporation, the S corporation, limited liability partnerships, and the tax-exempt nonprofit 501(c)3 corporation. For more information, read Chapters 18 and 20.

ESSENTIAL ENTREPRENEURIAL POWER SKILLS

If entrepreneurship is so compelling, why do so many people hesitate to start his or her first venture? Because they may be asking themselves this question:

Am I an entrepreneur?

Having coached thousands of students of entrepreneurship over the past 15 years, at all levels—from high school to advanced PhDs to executive education—you are not alone with this anxiety. This is the *wrong* question to ask, however, and one that leads to inaction. Entrepreneurship is not a "yes" or "no" phenomenon: "Yes, I'm an entrepreneur." "No, I'm not an entrepreneur." Entrepreneurship is not genetic. Entrepreneurship has nothing to do with your chromosomes or inherited traits. Entrepreneurs are not born; they make things happen because of their will to succeed and skills and knowledge. And you can learn and enhance the skills that make all entrepreneurs successful.

Ask yourself the *right* question:

> **How can I learn what I need to know, and improve my entrepreneurial skills to maximize my chances of succeeding?**

Successful entrepreneurs learn to develop and strengthen their personal power skills. Don't give up on yourself before realizing that you can develop these skills. Trust me: Becoming a successful entrepreneur is within your grasp if you really want to make it happen. The following list of the Essential Entrepreneurial Power Skills is excerpted from my book, *Trump University Entrepreneurship 101* (John Wiley & Sons, 2007):

1. *Assess the present situation.* Hone your ability to observe, collect information, and understand the opportunities and threats that can impact you

and your business-to-be. Factor in your own personal strengths, skills, experiences, challenges, and resource limitations. If you begin with the wrong assumptions, you will invariably get the wrong answers.

2. *Go after bold visions.* Having gone through a reasoned assessment, you are in a position to establish clear, measurable goals. Be bold! You can accomplish considerably more than you realize. And it takes about the same amount of effort to go for the gold.

3. *Be unstoppable.* Focus your attention on the timely execution of every milestone on the path to your goal. You and your team will face many obstacles along the way, but you will not let these stumbling blocks stop you. Just show up and get it done—period.

4. *Negotiate firmly and "win-winly."* Every interaction between people can benefit from proficiency at win-win negotiation. You can accomplish what you want and still retain a productive relationship based on mutual understanding and accommodation. Here are the ground rules:[1]
    *   Listen and understand, before seeking to be understood.
    *   Separate the people from the process.
    *   Focus on interests, not positions.
    *   Insist on objective criteria.
    *   Invent options for mutual gain.

    Win-win negotiating skills have been so important to me that I have included an entire chapter on this topic in my book *Trump University Entrepreneurship 101* (John Wiley & Sons, 2007).

5. *Solve problems effectively.* There is rarely a day in my business or personal life that a problem doesn't crop up that needs to be solved. Problem solving is a skill that can be learned through study[2] and practice. Start by identifying the problem meticulously, examine changes, test for causes, verify the solution. Your rate of success improves dramatically with your ability to solve problems.

6. *Make good decisions.* The ability to make good decisions is essential to success in business and personal life. Decision making can also be learned and enhanced.[3] The process begins with clarifying the decision statement; then defining what the right decision must accomplish; developing and evaluating alternatives; examining future consequences; and finally, making a reasoned choice. This is a process you can learn and apply to systematically improve your decision-making ability, as well as become a better problem solver. You don't have to wing it.

7. *Brainstorm.* Brainstorming harnesses the thinking, experiences, and imagination of a group to generate creative ideas and solve problems.

The collective knowledge of a group is vastly greater than that of any one individual; and therein lies the power of the brainstorming process.[4]

8. *Mobilize resources.* You can't accomplish anything without understanding how to leverage resources, which, in the entrepreneurial vocabulary, are anything, absolutely anything, that moves your venture further and faster with the least risk possible. Categories of resources include: physical, financial, infrastructure, people, knowledge, and your own unbridled imagination.

9. *Communicate.* You've assessed the situation, put your bold vision in place, and established performance initiatives. Now what happens? Nothing—unless you communicate consistently and constantly to all stakeholders. Be clear with stakeholders about what you intend to accomplish and what you expect from them.

10. *Act decisively.* Entrepreneurship is a contact sport. It is not only about thinking, planning, coordinating, strategizing, and visioning—it is about doing. Figure out how to get the task done. Be unstoppable in its execution.

11. *Behave with integrity.* There are people for whom you would do anything, and others with whom you would not waste your time; the difference is the quality of the person's character and behavior. Integrity, honesty, trustworthiness, reliability, knowledge, professionalism, maturity, punctuality, good negotiating and listening skills and, last but never least, humor, are the qualities of successful entrepreneurs. Stick to these and never waver.

Exhibit 10.1 on page 92 summarizes these eleven needed skills and assists you in assessing your own strengths and challenges. To assist you in building your Essential Entrepreneurial Power Skills, visit www.trumpuniversity.com/wealthbuilding101 to download Exhibit 10.1.

OVERCOMING OBSTACLES

Deep down, you may want to be in business for yourself, but there are real—and perceived—obstacles and risks. Remember, entrepreneurship is a trial-and-error activity; the more times you try, the more you learn, and the better you get at rebounding. As mentioned earlier, my own track record includes 11 attempted start-ups, but only 6 resulted in businesses that produced operating cash flow.

Downloadable Exhibit 10.1   Essential Entrepreneurial Power Skills*

Essential Entrepreneurial Power Skills	Self-Assessment Least 1 – 2 – 3 – 4 – 5 Best	Action to Improve
Assess the present situation		
Go after bold visions		
Be unstoppable		
Negotiate firmly and "win-winly"		
Solve problems effectively		
Make good decisions		
Brainstorm		
Mobilize resources		
Communicate		
Act decisively		
Behave with integrity		

Note: A blank version of this exhibit can be downloaded from www.trumpuniversity.com/wealth building101 for your personal use.

Source: www.CompetitiveSuccess.com, "Essential Entrepreneurial Power Skills." Copyright © 2005 by Michael E. Gordon. Used with permission.

The solution to obstacles and risks? Learn to control all risks, so that nonsuccess in pursuing one opportunity doesn't put you out of the game permanently.

Try this: When you come across successful entrepreneurs at your health club, networking meetings, or other business and social events, ask them about their entrepreneurial histories. Repeatedly, you will hear that most, and perhaps all, did not succeed on their first attempt. They kept going, repositioned their first opportunity or abandoned it, and began exploring another.

This classic vignette about Thomas Edison epitomizes this point:

Thomas Edison, the greatest inventor of all time (1,093 patents for such inventions as the phonograph, the stock tickertape machine, medical x-ray devices, and carbon telephone transmitter, to name a few) was attempting to develop a filament for the electric lightbulb. He and his team conducted more than

8,000 experiments, trying all sorts of materials, and under every imaginable condition. An acquaintance is said to have asked, "Mr. Edison, how can you keep going in the face of 8,000 failures? Why aren't you crushed by the futility and frustration?" Edison replied coolly, "I never had one failure. I learned from every attempt, and each experiment led me to more likely pathways, and I will eventually succeed." Lights on!

What obstacles are holding you back? Instead of letting them prevent you from achieving your entrepreneurial success, think of obstacles as calls to action. For example:

1. *Lack of financial resources:* Soften this obstacle immediately by asking yourself what action you should take. Where should you look for start-up capital? How can you proceed so that money does not stop or limit you? What do you have to do to move forward with your limited financial resources? How much money will you need to launch and grow your venture? This obstacle presents an excellent opportunity to brainstorm with your friends and advisors.

2. *Potential for financial loss:* Keep Edison's "Trying Game" in mind. Invest carefully in what you believe is an opportunity. If your venture does not make it, the next time you attempt a start-up, you will be more savvy and your chances of succeeding are greater. Don't make major expenditures until you have confidence that you are on the scent of a real opportunity. Specifically, what amounts of financial loss are you worried about? At what point might your business not make it, and how much money in total will you lose in the worst case? Are we talking about a life-threatening amount, or a sum that you would be willing to lose to explore a chance of a lifetime?

   The short answer is: Don't put the future of your family or yourself at risk. If we are talking about sacrificing a new SUV ($35,000), a family vacation ($15,000), two cups of coffee a day ($1,750 annually), cigarette smoking ($1,500 annually), chocolate chip cookies (now that would be a huge sacrifice for me!), or (fill in your own sacrifice here), you may be willing to make such a sacrifice.

   To find money for your start-up:
   • Bootstrap to minimize costs. Be a penny pincher.
   • Mobilize free resources, equipment, and people.
   • Develop your business during evenings and weekends.
   • Spend the minimum on development and start-up costs until you know you are on the right track.

- Get one or more partners.
- Brainstorm with others.

3. *Career Risks such as Loss of Income and Loss of Work Environment:* This is an easy one. If you succeed in building your own profitable money machine, you create the most fantastic, tailor-made career imaginable. You also select your own community of coworkers.

    In my second business, I wanted to handle international marketing, and still run the company as CEO. Building a strong organizational infrastructure was needed—one that could function without me for periods of time while I was traveling. What more could I have wanted—traveling the globe, running international trade shows, and meeting with distributors and customers around the world? It would have been quite unlikely for me to have gotten that kind of ideal job without being my own boss. But don't quit your day job until you are confident that your opportunity is real, and your resources are ready and available.

4. *Lack of self-confidence:* Self-confidence comes from succeeding, so go for it. If you don't jump into the Trying Game, you will go through life feeling the absence of self-esteem.

    If your first few attempts are nonsuccesses, your self-perception will increase because of what you have learned. Take courage and keep trying, like Thomas Edison, and, if you do—like Edison—you will succeed. Just go carefully and watch your cash flow.

5. *Pressure on the family:* For me, it was really important to find a balance between my entrepreneurial pursuit and my strong family passion. When I was starting my first business, my children were young. My father had died during that period also, and my entire family needed emotional support. I tried to involve the family in my activities where possible, and I looked for creative ways to spend family time, collectively and individually. Awareness and sensitivity make it possible to find the balance.

6. *Health, stress, long hours:* Whenever you are getting burnt out, relax. Find the balance!

    Exercise, eat healthy, unwind with family and friends, get involved in activities, meditate, sing, play, listen to music, laugh, dance, go to movies, read . . . but don't lose sight of your entrepreneurial focus.

7. *Lack of the big opportunity:* Opportunity is a central theme in entrepreneurship. You must search for ideas, screen out the losers, and identify the potential winning opportunities. In the next chapter, we'll talk about how to do this in greater detail.

8. *Minimal tolerance for risk:* Ask yourself what specific risks are intolerable. Separate them into small pieces so you can gain clarity. You need to take risks to accomplish your entrepreneurial dreams, but you can manage these risks, and put them in perspective.

   There are a few ways to look at risk tolerance. Here is Gordon's 1-in-5,000 rule. My passion is traveling and experiencing the wonders of our world, so years ago, I asked myself, "What is my risk tolerance for flying? What if one plane in one million goes down? One in 100,000? One in 1,000? One in 100?" I concluded that my risk comfort zone for flying is about 1 in 5,000, because living with absolute fear and zero risk tolerance would prevent me from pursuing my passion for travel. What kind of a life would that be? To me, none at all. Ask yourself, "What is the risk I'm willing to take, for the reward of pursuing my entrepreneurial career?"

9. *Inertia.* This happens to everyone. Brainstorm with friends. Ask them to help you define your inertia. Reexamine your goals.

   Personally, when I get stuck, my frustration goes sky high and *I have to do something!* That's my advice to you—do something! Take one extremely frugal step in any likely entrepreneurial direction. Action will lead you out of the wilderness.

10. *I still don't think I have what it takes to be an entrepreneur:* Not true!!—As mentioned earlier, everyone has the potential to learn and enhance their 11 Essential Entrepreneurial Power Skills.

    As your toolbox of traits becomes stronger, you may gain the confidence to jump into the Trying Game. At the very least, you will feel more in control of your life, and eventually, your entrepreneurial passions may grab hold of you and drive you toward the start-up of your own business.

This chapter speaks to the achievement of your entrepreneurial dream. It speaks of great courage, unbridled passion, laser focus, and massive commitment. I'll leave you with these words from the author and poet J.W. von Goethe:

Until one is committed, there is hesitancy, the chance to draw back, always ineffectiveness . . . Whatever you can do or dream you can, begin it. Boldness has genius, power and magic in it. Begin it now.

11

START YOUR OWN BUSINESS
by
Michael E. Gordon, PhD

In the last chapter, you learned the two compelling reasons to pursue a career in entrepreneurship: (1) realizing your personal potential and (2) creating wealth. This chapter demystifies entrepreneurship and guides you through the process of identifying business opportunities and creating a new venture. Starting your own business will be the most exhilarating and challenging journey that you can imagine. Passion, single-minded focus, and hard, smart work will carry the day. Take the following steps one at a time, and by the seventh and last, step, you will have turned on your money machine:

Step 1. Search for many business ideas.

Step 2. Select the one most promising opportunity.

Step 3. Develop an effective executive summary.

Step 4. Create your business identity.

Step 5. Build your milestone charts.

Step 6. Mobilize resources.

Step 7. Capture that first magic customer.

Step 1: Search for Many Business Ideas

Most entrepreneurs assume that their creative idea can be commercialized expeditiously into a profitable business. Not so! Ideas are only the starting point, and every idea must go through a rigorous evaluation and selection process. You must separate the lumps of coal from the few diamonds in the rough. Ideas and opportunities are not the same, and you need to understand the difference. If your idea is not an opportunity, not one minute, not one dollar should be spent on it—it's a nonstarter. If you are uncertain, proceed cautiously, with small, frugal learning steps until the yes or no answer emerges clearly. But if you are sure that you have an opportunity, then step on the gas and use the rest of this chapter as your guide to success.

How do you know if you have a winning idea? Consider this example. My wife, Maria Alejandra, was interested in being in her own business, so one bright spring day, we walked around town exploring businesses that appealed to her. I challenged her to look at every business on our itinerary and ask herself these three questions:

1. Is this a good business?
2. Is this a business that will capture my passions?
3. Is this a business where I can add unique customer value?

Maria took up the challenge with gusto, and many more questions danced in her mind. We walked past at least 50 businesses that morning. These included: a pizza shop, beauty salon, clothing store, jewelry store, copy center, antiques consignment store, newspaper and magazine store, Mexican food restaurant, flower shop, an office supplies store, an optician, sushi restaurant, coffee shop, used bookstore, hardware store, and many, many more. None interested her, and few seemed to have much potential for future growth.

Then, suddenly, Maria spotted an interesting shop that sold an incredible variety of beads and patterns to do-it-yourself jewelry makers for necklaces, earrings, handbags, hats, and gloves. We went inside and observed. We made mental notes on the number of customers, their ages, gender, time of day, and what they were buying. Then we bought some items and stood near the cash register to determine the size of each sale. We counted the number of sales over a 30-minute period.

Later, over coffee in a nearby restaurant, we projected the hourly, daily, weekly, and annual sales of the bead shop. We "guesstimated" that sales for that location exceeded $500,000 annually, and that profit margins before expenses were about 50 percent; that is, every $100 of bead sales cost the business $50 in labor and materials. The business was attractive from several perspectives: repeat customers, nonperishable inventory, excellent location, potential for growth through additional locations, and, finally, the fact that it was a simple business to understand. Also, Maria felt that the business would engage her artistic talents, and she liked the community of artistic people who were attracted to the store.

Then the most exciting thing of all happened: Maria said, "If I owned that shop, I would create a tight community of beading enthusiasts. They could hang out in my shop and share their beading interests in a comfortable social environment with coffee, tea, and snacks. I might call it The Beading Café, and have guest speakers, craft shows, and a consignment store as well. It would be the best beading shop in the area." Maria's creative juices were really flowing. She was thinking about how to add unique value for her customers. Not bad for a two-hour walk!

This simple exercise presents an entrepreneurial model for how you can search out and test a winning idea. Imagine a funnel. By walking around our neighborhood, Maria filled the top of the funnel with 50 or more business ideas, and then used her own judgment to screen out those that didn't fit her. But fit alone is not enough; fit is only the starting point. Maria got her creative juices going, and found her comfortable fit when she realized she could add value. Maria's idea will need to go through much more rigorous scrutiny using the Opportunity Screening Checklist, included a little later in this chapter.

IDEAS CAN COME FROM ANYWHERE

An idea for a new venture can come from absolutely anywhere. My own approach to idea generation is **P**roactive, **E**nergetic, and **P**urposeful—PEP.

When the weather is accommodating, I jog or ride my bike around my extended neighborhood and keep my eyes open for real estate development opportunities. At the very least, I have a pleasant experience. At the very best, I spot an idea that may turn into a good business opportunity. Recently, I identified two properties worth exploring this way. I also work with three realtors who are always on the lookout for me.

To search for businesses for sale, I frequently check out brokerservice network.com, and also attend stock investment meetings to learn about high-potential, small public companies below the radar screen.

The concept of the idea funnel is burned into my subconscious. For a few good ideas to pop out of the bottom of the funnel, I know that 50 to 100 ideas need to go into the top. Here are my 10 favorite idea hunting grounds:

1. Wherever my passions lead me.
2. Any trade show in an attractive industry.
3. Real estate and business opportunities that I read about in newspapers including: the *Banker and Tradesman*, *Investor's Business Daily*, and the *Wall Street Journal*.
4. Franchising shows.
5. The best practices of other companies.
6. Magazines and catalogues such as *Inc.*, *Entrepreneur*, *MIT Technology Review*, *Popular Electronics*, and *PC World*
7. Unstoppable world trends: energy shortages; the commercialization of Asia; population/demographics; the increasing U.S. national debt; global warming; the liftoff of digital, wireless, mobile, and personal devices.
8. Brainstorming with my entrepreneurial friends.
9. Attending business and technology networking meetings where entrepreneurs and investors gather.
10. Spending time at local bookstores and browsing current books about Web revenue models.

Pause here. Take a few minutes and generate your own list of idea hunting grounds.

Step 2: Select the One Most Promising Opportunity

There is a world of difference between a promising idea and a profitable entrepreneurial opportunity. Earlier, we looked at my wife Maria's idea strictly for personal "fit" between her objectives, skills, risk tolerance, and passions. That was the easy part. Now her idea must overcome many more demanding hurdles. Exhibit 11.1 provides an outline of the multidimensional factors shown to characterize entrepreneurial opportunities.[1] As you go through the checklist, look at where each factor falls on a scale from 1 to 5 (5 being the most attractive). Your goal is to arrive at a Go/No-Go decision about whether to commit resources to pursue your *one* opportunity.

Downloadable Exhibit 11.1   Opportunity Screening Checklist*

Category	Opportunity Screening Checklist	Rating/Comments 1 2 3 4 5 Low High
Personal fit	Is there a fit between your idea and your personal skills, passions, risk tolerance, and objectives?	
Value to customers	Does your product or service eliminate a nagging problem for your customer? Is it unique, innovative, or creative? Does it add significant, cost-effective value for your customer?	
Market dynamics	Is the market large and growing? Is the industry favorable in terms of competitors, buyers, suppliers, substitutes, and future entrants? Can you gain market share because of an untapped market niche, weak and frag-mented competitors, and reachable customers?	
Profitability and scalability	Is there a strong and profitable customer need, want, and demand? Is there the potential for recurring profitable sales? How sensitive is the market to product pricing? Can you reach break-even sales and positive cash flow rapidly?	
Financial issues	Do you have sufficient financial resources to start and grow your business? Is your business capable of generating an attractive and timely return on investment (ROI) for yourself and for other investors?	
Management team	Do you and your team have industry knowledge, skills, experience, and strong entrepreneurial traits? Are you unstoppable?	

Competitive advantages and differentiators	Where will your competitive advantages come from (e.g., product/service uniqueness, lowest cost provider, entry into an untapped market niche, strong customer relationships, access to channels of distribution, unique competencies, proprietary know-how, barriers to future competitor threats, first mover advantage)? Do you have an opportunity based on inexorable trends, such as global market expansion, energy shortages, disruptive technology, new business methodology, the disruption of your competitors through the application of information technology, channels of outsourcing, resource shortages, or others?	
Fatal Flaws (defects that cannot be changed)	Are there particular defects in your business that cannot be surmounted—overpowering competition, cost of market entry, small size of market, lack of customer need/want, inability to deliver products and services at acceptable prices, or others?	

Note: A blank version of this exhibit can be downloaded from www.trumpuniversity.com/wealthbuilding101 for your personal use.

This is an important checklist. Pause here. Mark this page and put each one of your ideas and potential opportunities through this checklist. Reach a Go/No-Go decision.

Step 3: Develop an Effective Executive Summary

Once you have identified a bona fide opportunity, you are on your way. No journey of any consequence, however, begins without a plan; the same applies to starting and operating a business. If you want to get where you intend to go, you need a road map. Without it, the outcome of all your labors will be strictly random—and probably disappointing. Generally a business plan is a lengthy document and the product of a great deal of research and effort. At this point, however, you don't need a complete business plan; a mini-plan or Executive Summary is enough. Here is an example of an effective Executive Summary for The Beading Café, excerpted from my book, *Trump University Entrepreneurship 101* (Hoboken, NJ: John Wiley & Sons, 2007).

The Beading Café

Executive Summary

January, 2008

The Company

The Beading Café is a new company that will provide a community environment for avid bead lovers of all skill levels. Located in Brookline Village, the company will offer regular and frequent classes, and will sell a comprehensive selection of beads from around the world, tools, findings, supplies, and finished beaded jewelry from our own inventory and on consignment.

Our value proposition for our customers is based on the creation of a magnetic, aesthetic, friendly atmosphere. Repeat customers will come for the camaraderie, for the learning experience, and to create their own beautiful beadwork. In a gracious 2,000 square-foot setting, supplies and work tables will be available, in addition to continuous free tea, honey, mint, and lemon. Sandwiches, salads, gourmet coffees, pastries, and other snacks will be available for sale. Skilled teachers will be retained on an as-needed basis. When classes are not being held, videos will be shown so that regular customers can learn on their own as they purchase the needed supplies. There will be background music for aesthetics. The company will expand through acquisitions, new stores, and franchises.

Our Mission

To build a profitable chain of beading stores based on a social, creative, learning atmosphere.

Keys to Success

- Implementing a winning concept based on a magnetic culture of camaraderie, beading, and aesthetics.
- Marketing, marketing, marketing, and more marketing.

- Capturing very desirable locations and expanding through acquisitions, starting new stores, and franchising.
- Mobilizing financial resources for new locations.

Market Characteristics

The retail beading business is a regional and fragmented market. Competition is local, and there are no dominant branded beading competitors. There are 10 beading stores in our geographic market within a 10-mile radius. What is missing in this attractive and profitable beading market is a social community environment. As the first mover, we will have a short-term advantage. Other competitors will be able to copy our best practices and to replicate our concept. However, through an aggressive local advertising and promotion program, we intend to capture market share quickly. Once captured, the customers would be ours, and we would not take them for granted.

Competition

Competitors	Location	Social	Supplies	Classes	Café
The Beading Café	Brookline	Yes	Yes	Yes	Yes
Bead Company of America	Cambridge, Boston	No	Yes	Yes	No
Red Crystal	Watertown	No	Yes	Yes	No
Beads Boston	Newton	No	Yes	No	No
Beautiful Creations	Winthrop	No	Yes	No	No
Ancient Stars	Watertown	No	Yes	No	No
Belle Art Supplies	Newton	No	Yes	No	No
Rose Garden	Brookline	No	Yes	No	No
Bini's Tree House	Boston	No	Yes	No	No
Personal Jewels	Cambridge	No	Yes	No	No

The Team

The company has a strong management team of two seasoned beading enthusiasts with extensive experience in, and knowledge of, the beading business.

Maria Alejandra Figaredo, CEO, brings extensive aesthetic and operational experience to this present position, as well as 15 years as a beading hobbyist. She worked part time as a supervisor in a jewelry store in

Houston for three years and understands the operations and supply chain. She has run beading classes in her home for the past six years and has developed advanced beading skills. Her entrepreneurial enthusiasm and well-grounded background will enable her to build this chain of beading stores.

Jeanne Gordon, Vice President, Marketing, is an accomplished jewelry artist. Her passion is to design, make, and sell unique jewelry from precious metals, minerals, and beads. Her marketing skills have enabled her to establish a consignment arts and crafts business locally and over the Internet that has been profitable for many years.

Financial Projections (All Financial Numbers is $000)

	2008	2009	2010	2011	2012
Total number of locations	1	1	1	2	3
Revenue streams					
Product sales	110	180	320	500	650
Classes	30	60	80	120	250
Food/beverages	40	80	100	230	300
Total revenue	180	320	500	850	1,200
Cost of goods sold	90	160	250	425	600
Earnings from operations	8	36	55	94	140
Financing needs	100	—	—	200	250

Investment Summary

Several factors have resulted in an attractive opportunity for The Beading Café:

- The management team is strong, motivated, and experienced. Both partners bring operational, marketing, and artistic talent to the business.
- Revenue will come from four sources: supplies, classes, food, and online sales.
- Profits will grow as other locations are opened, franchised, or acquired. Higher profits will result from economies of scale for inventory, as well as from uniform financial and operational control systems.
- Profit margins are attractive and will improve with each new store opening.
- Timeliness. No competitor has emerged to fill this niche for a social and aesthetic beading café environment.

The Beading Café

302 Cary Ave., Brookline, MA 02020
Tel: (617)890-XXXX Fax: (617) 890-YYYY
www.TheBeadingCafé.com

Suggestion: Pause here and mark this page. If you already have identified an opportunity, use The Beading Café as a template to build your own Executive Summary. This brief document will significantly reduce your risks and increase your chance of success.

Step 4: Create Your Business Identity

Let me use one of my own ventures as an example. AngelDeals.com is a virtual business whose mission is to help entrepreneurs find funding over the Internet, by giving them access to venture capital and "angel" investor databases, as well as business planning tutorials and checklists.

To create my business identity, I went to www.GoDaddy.com to find a domain name for my venture. Since the goal of my network was to connect entrepreneurs with private or "angel," investors, I registered the name AngelDeals.com. Then I went to City Hall in Boston and paid $50 for a business permit to do business in Boston under that name (a DBA, or Doing Business As). Later, with help from a business lawyer, I would establish the company as a C corporation, S corporation, a limited liability company, or a nonprofit 501(c)(3) business. (In Chapter 20, "Protect Your Assets," J. J. Childers explains the steps in detail to choosing and forming the right business structure.) Also check out the library, and http://smallbusiness.findlaw.com/business-structures/business-structures-quickstart.html. I strongly recommend that you seek the services of a business lawyer and accountant regarding the formation of your business.

Next, I went to a local bank and opened a checking account in my name, doing business as AngelDeals.com. I deposited $500 into this free checking account and ordered free checks. Then I went to a local office supply store and ordered professional-looking business cards. Finally, I created the format for letterhead and envelopes in Microsoft Word. In less than five hours, I had my identity. Why is this important for you? The identity grows on you, and every time you hand out a business card, or send a letter or e-mail, or write a check, you are telling the world: Here comes my business! As you grow into your new identity, you become unstoppable.

STEP 5: BUILD YOUR MILESTONE CHARTS

Milestone charts define all the key events that must occur before you start your venture. In all of my endeavors, I have found it essential to visualize what needed to be done on a daily, weekly, monthly, and yearly basis. Exhibit 11.2 shows the first milestone chart for the development and start up of AngelDeals.com.

Take particular note of the arrows. They keep you focused, so you don't lose sight of the timing to reach your primary goal. Each milestone tells you what to do and when to do it. If you miss one milestone, the prompt becomes a roar. Tape these charts on the wall over your desk. It's hard to be in denial when this chart stares back at you.

Exhibit 11. 2   Milestone Chart for the Start Up of AngelDeals.com

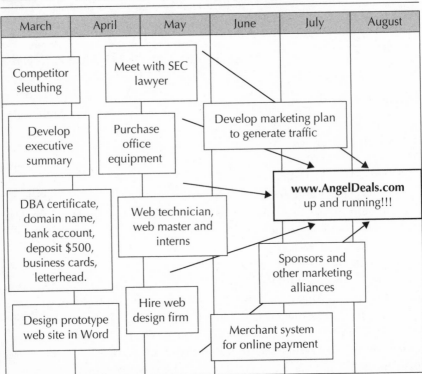

Source: The Center for Competitive Success, "Milestone Chart for the Start Up of AngelDeals. com." Copyright © 2005 by Michael E. Gordon, For permission, contact the author at www. CompetitiveSuccess.com.

The resource list for the start-up of AngelDeals.com looked like Exhibit 11.3. You will be well-rewarded if you pay particular attention to mobilizing the most effective resources. Without sufficient resources, you will not be able to accomplish the needed tasks on time and to the highest levels of achievement.

STEP 6: MOBILIZE RESOURCES

Downloadable Exhibit 11.3   Needed Resources for the Start-Up of AngelDeals.com*

Start-Up Resources	Source	Use of Funds

**Note:* A blank version of this exhibit can be downloaded from www.trumpuniversity.com/wealthbuilding101 for your personal use.

Source: www.Competitive Success.com. "Needed Resources for the Start-Up of AngelDeals. com." Copyright © 2000 by Michael E. Gordon. Reprinted with permission.

STEP 7: CAPTURE THAT FIRST MAGIC CUSTOMER

Now you are ready for the big time—capturing your first customer! When you do, everyone thinks differently about you and your business. You are no longer a development-stage company. You are an early-stage operating company. You had your vision from the beginning. You went through the many, and often, tortuous, steps in the entrepreneurial process, and now it is all coming to fruition. Before your first customer, you were untried, but now, that one customer brings everything together. Your credibility goes sky high.

I can recall vividly the exact moment in my first business when I captured my first customer. An honest-to-goodness purchasing agent sent an order for $2,700 to build a prototype for their company. Words cannot describe my exuberance. I began to notice the change in my own focus. I was not starting the company any more; I was thinking about how to fill this order and how to capture more customers.

If that first paying customer is so magical, how can you capture him? Brainstorm. Bring together a group of imaginative, positive, and willing stakeholders and friends to help you invent ways to capture your first customer. Here are examples:

- Use "guerrilla marketing"[2] to get your first customer. This term refers to using inexpensive, unusual, brash, and visible publicity methods to gain a "huge bang for the buck." Personally hand out brochures and flyers; get referrals from friends, colleagues, or other contacts; spend money on an effective marketing and advertising campaign.
- Customize the product for the customer with no obligation on her part. Make it worth her while. Tell her that if she likes the product or service, and places the order, you want to feature her testimonial in a publication.
- Take the first order at the most nominal price you can afford. If you have a retail store, discount 50 percent off the list price to the first 100 customers. Offer a free trial for one month, with no obligation to buy. Give serious guarantees: money back, no ifs, ands, or buts.
- Use the concept of the sales funnel. For every 100 possible leads that go into the mouth of the funnel, if 10 percent are interested—and only one becomes a purchase order—you have succeeded. If you can improve your conversion rate at each step, you are on your way to a real success.
- Harness your unstoppable personal power—whatever you have to do to get that first customer.

With this as a starter list, continue to brainstorm. Your first customer will happen. Guaranteed!

Starting and growing your own business is a journey through each of the seven steps described in this chapter. Properly completed, each step will bring you closer to your goal: building a profitable money machine that will provide prosperity and self-esteem. With this chapter as a guide, you are on your way to creating significant wealth through entrepreneurship.

12

BUY YOUR OWN BUSINESS
by
Richard Parker

If you have to work, you may as well work for yourself.! It's no secret that if you want to accumulate wealth, you won't get rich working for someone else. But I'll let you in on a big secret: *Making the leap from employee to employer is a lot easier than you might think.*

The beauty of owning your own business is:

- You take complete control of your financial future.
- You get paid for the work you produce.
- You build value in the business, which one day you sell for a lot of money.
- You create a better lifestyle for yourself and your family.

Many people don't see a direct link between the hard work they do and the compensation they receive, and they don't like the fact that their future depends on a boss, a company's overall performance, or fickle shareholders.

The idea of buying a business may seem like a dream, but it's not. If you take the specific steps I'm going to share, prepare yourself properly, and navigate carefully through the business-buying process, you, too, can own the business of your dreams.

In 1990, when I bought my first business, I didn't have the luxury of a guide. I was earning $100,000 a year working in the consumer products division of a large company when I lost $60,000 in the stock market. I was frantic—my first child was on the way. The only way I could get out of the hole was to win the Lottery, or go into my own business.

Sometimes I made mistakes, but with each new acquisition, I learned and began to recognize these eight key steps to success:

1. Find the right business for you.
2. Know where to search.
3. Visit the business and meet with the seller.
4. Value the business.
5. Negotiate the deal.
6. Finance the purchase.
7. Do your own due diligence.
8. Close the deal.

Be prepared to work very hard. In the beginning, I put in over 60 hours a week, and I was always thinking about my business.

Is it worth it? Absolutely! From day one of buying my first business, I scheduled my work so that I had the time I wanted to spend with my children, and time to go fly fishing every Wednesday afternoon. It's about the money, but it's also about more than the money. That's why I call my business DIOMO, for "Doing It On My Own."

STEP 1: FIND THE RIGHT BUSINESS FOR YOU

Be very honest with yourself about your strengths and weaknesses. The right business will grow from your strengths, and not suffer from your weaknesses. Never, ever buy a business simply because you like the product. You love birds, but that doesn't mean you're qualified to run an exotic bird store where marketing may be the biggest skill that you need.

Whatever you do best must be the single most important driving factor of the sales and profits of any business you're thinking about buying. I'll use an example to illustrate:

Margaret was an attorney by education. When she decided to buy a local moving and storage business, she had zero experience in the field, the industry had an awful reputation, and men controlled the business almost exclusively at every level.

Her greatest strength, what she did best—dealing with people and making them comfortable and willing to trust her—was the "driver" to her success. Margaret realized that most people don't like moving companies, and she understood a key issue: In most households, the woman takes charge of a family's move and doesn't like dealing with slick salesmen or truck drivers. So Margaret hired females to handle every sales call and to be at the initial meeting. In less than five years, sales grew from $1 million to $7 million, and profit zoomed from $200,000 to almost $2 million.

Ask yourself these questions, and be very honest:

- What am I good at? What are my greatest strengths? My greatest weaknesses?
- What type of business will grow from my strengths? What businesses don't I want?
- How much money do I need to earn from day one? What do I expect?
- Can I manage employees? Do I prefer dealing with the public, or directly with businesses?
- What industry do I know best? Is there a certain niche I can exploit? In what professional roles did I experience my greatest successes?
- What am I willing to sacrifice for the business? Do I have any restrictions?

Your answers become the basis of your "Golden Rules" that you must apply every time you visit a business. Over the years, I've found that five Golden Rules are not too much, or too little, to use in judging a good prospect. Here are my five Golden Rules:

1. The business must be sales- and marketing-driven.
2. The business must have some element of exclusivity. For example, the product or services sold are-sold only within a certain protected territory.
3. The business must have a product or service with a high gross margin, which will allow me to fund various activities to drive the business, and give me a cushion for a few mistakes along the way.
4. There must be built-in demand for the product or service being offered.
5. Business products or services can't compete solely on price.

You must develop your own rules—it is critical. Your Golden Rules must be specific. Don't say, "I want to spend more time with my family." Say, "The business has to take my time from Monday to Friday only."

Over the years, I've added a sixth and seventh rule:

6. Buy businesses with few employees.
7. Generate repeat business from the same client base.

I'm willing to forfeit Rule 6 or Rule 7, but I won't compromise—ever—on my Five Golden Rules. You can't, either.

STEP 2: KNOW WHERE TO SEARCH

Once you know what's right for you, finding the right business is easy. Most people search endless listings of businesses for sale trying to figure out which, if any, is right for them. That's the wrong approach. Rule out ones you don't want and focus on the others. There are a number of sources for locating businesses that are for sale.

Online

Online sources such as www.bizquest.com, www.bizbuysell.com, and www. businessesforsale.com act as a clearinghouse for businesses that are for sale. Search with keywords such as, "business for sale" or "buy a business," and search local, city, and state areas. In the listing, you'll find business description and location, asking price and down payment, owner benefits (Seller Cash Flow, or Adjusted Earnings, what the business generates), training, contact information, and who is selling the business (the seller, or a broker).

Don't ask for a lot of information in the initial contact. Instead, state: "I am interested in this business, and I am a serious buyer. Please send me the necessary confidentiality agreements to sign so we can proceed." Then make a note of the listing number and the web site, if you don't hear back within 48 hours, contact them again.

Newspapers

Choices may be fewer than online, but check your local paper regularly, usually under "Business Opportunities," in the classified section.

Trade Publications

Most people overlook these. Once you know what type of business you want to buy, get a copy of the industry publications and scour the classifieds.

Whenever you speak to a seller, find out the trade journals relevant to the business, and read those, too.

Business Brokers

Business brokers do not operate the same way as real estate agents, and not all states have multiple listings. In fact, there are very few brokers who work for buyers; in almost all cases, they're paid by, and represent, the seller, or the deal. That said, they can be helpful to a buyer.

Accountants and Attorneys

Network with as many accountants and attorneys as possible. They may have clients with businesses they want to sell. Research them and send a letter to all of them introducing yourself and letting them know what type of business interests you.

Friends, Family, and Other Resources

Get the word out. Buying a business is like searching for a job—you've got to pull out all the stops. Leverage your network—your family, your friends, and your banker. Attend Chamber of Commerce meetings and local trade shows. You never know when, or how, the right lead will surface.

Direct Solicitations

Contact business owners directly. Do this once you know the industry and type of business you want to acquire. Usually I ask an accountant or attorney to send out a letter on his or her stationery, because it looks more impressive. Provide a contact number, so the accountant or attorney does not have to field your calls. Or send out your own letter. For more information, check out my Ten Commandments at www.trumpuniversity.com/wealthbuilding101.com.

STEP 3: VISIT THE BUSINESS AND MEET WITH THE SELLER

This is the best way to narrow the list to the *right* business for you, and to fine-tune your Golden Rules. You can't buy a business from an ad. You need to speak with sellers and visit with them to really learn about their business.

Every potential buyer needs to ask key questions. Here are just a few:

- Can you give me an overview of the business?
- Why are you selling?
- Can you elaborate on the terms of sale?
- Would you stay on and train me longer than indicated in the Listing Agreement, or can I hire you as a consultant?
- What are the biggest challenges facing the business in the future?
- What keeps you up at night?
- Are there any obligations, contractual or verbal, with any employees?
- Do you like the business?
- Who are your main competitors and how can I get more information about them?
- What are the resources available to me?
- Do you have a business or marketing plan?
- Why do your customers buy from you? Do any represent more than 10 percent of the business?
- How much salary and benefit, including vacation, do you take?
- If you were starting out again, what would you do differently?
- If money wasn't an issue, as a new owner, what would you do, specifically, to grow the business?

Then be prepared for questions they'll ask you, such as:

- What is your background?
- What is your area of expertise?
- What is your financial situation?
- What is your time line to buy a business?

Keep your answers brief, and stick to the point.

Next Steps

After the meeting, ask yourself: "Do I like the seller? Do I trust him or her? Do I like the business? Can I see myself running it?"

If you can't answer yes to all of these questions, move on. Be sure to send a note to the broker or seller thanking them for their time. They may be a source of valuable future leads.

Step 4: Value the Business

Now the fun begins. What a seller thinks his business is worth usually has nothing to do with the value. Valuation is an art, not a science. Forget the asking price. A sound valuation includes doing the following:

- Review past financials.
- Achieve an adequate return on your investment.
- Determine how the business will transition to a new owner.
- Understand any inherent problems in the business (e.g., too few customers generate too much business).
- And finally, estimate realistic growth potential.

There are many valuation methods, but with most small business acquisitions, the multiple method is used to determine the valuation company's financials. Use the "Total Owner Benefits," which assumes everything remains status quo after you buy: how much the business will generate to pay your salary, service the debt, and build the business.

Here's the formula:

$$\text{Net income} + \text{Owner salary} + \text{Owner perks} + \text{Interest} + \text{Depreciation} - \text{Capital expenditures} = \text{Total owner benefits}$$

Look at two to three years of these figures. Here is an example:

Net income (off the tax return):	$80,000
Owner salary:	$70,000
Owner perks:[1]	$50,000
Depreciation:	$20,000
Interest:	$5,000
TOTAL:	$225,000
Less Capital expenditure allowance:[2]	($25,000)
TOTAL:	**$200,000**

[1] Owner perks can include medical insurance, a spouse's car, personal vacations, or meals charged to the business.

[2] On average, the company spends $25,000 annually to replace old equipment, so you must deduct this.

Say the seller is asking for $600,000, three times the Owner benefit. Most small businesses are valued from one to three times, so that is on the high side. Is the business worth that? If the business can continue to grow, and the deal terms make sense, it can be. That is why you need to review all parts of the business, financial and otherwise, to arrive at a proper valuation.

To download a terrific valuation tool, check out "Valuing a Business" from my *Art of Buying a Business,* at www.trumpuniversity.com/wealthbuilding101.

Step 5: Negotiate the Deal

The negotiating stage tells you a lot about the seller. Certain issues must be covered in any acquisition. Engage an attorney experienced in transactional law for small business sales. The attorney will provide counsel and make sure you are properly protected, but the majority of the negotiations will be done between you and the seller.

Win-win sounds great in theory, but it's not always practical in the sale of a business. As the buyer, who is assuming greater risk, you should win, but the seller should be reasonably happy, too. Understand the seller's "hot buttons" and satisfy them, and he or she will give you everything you want. If you reach a stalemate on one point, move on to the next, and come back if necessary. Only take a hard stand if you're prepared to walk away from the deal. Don't be a wimp, but don't be a bully either. Look at the following example:

> Edward was buying a distribution company. Stan, the seller, and his wife Lynette, wanted to retire. He had a terrific business, one that a smart buyer could easily grow. Stan and his wife were offering a very fair price and terms, but Edward kept coming back to the table for more and more, right up to the closing. He pummeled and pushed the seller on every point, and never gave in.
>
> On the last day, as the final documents were being signed and the money being transferred, Edward told Stan: "I can't wait to get in and get rid of Stella" (Stan's longtime, and less-than-exceptional assistant). Stan snapped. "I've let you push me around since we met. I gave in to every point. Shove your money and sue me if you want. I'm not selling to you." And he walked out.
>
> Edward was shocked. He lost a gem of a business. Four months later, Stan and Lynette sold for more money to another buyer.

In a typical agreement, there are 50 individual clauses to negotiate. I'll discuss a few of them next.

Price and Terms

These include the price of the business, the down payment, the financing terms, and the deal structure. For example, in cases where there is a customer concentration issue, business is declining, or there is the "promise" of a big contract, the deal can be structured as a performance-based purchase or earn-out, which means the seller gets a premium for certain events that materialize or continue after you take over.

What Assets Are You Buying?

Be clear about what assets come with the purchase of the business, and if they're "free and clear," including equipment, company web site, patents, copyrights, and others, and any other intangible assets.

Asset or Stock Sale

Unless the deal involves the transfer of specific business licenses or contracts, structure the deal as an asset purchase and not as a stock sale. You can then "step up" the assets and depreciate them again, which is a major tax advantage, and also avoids any liability you would inherit in a stock purchase.

Noncompete

This clause prevents the seller from going back into business and competing with you for a certain period of time and distance.

Customer or Supplier Concentration Issues

You will need protection and a remedy to deal with these issues. As described in "Price and Terms", earnouts are a great mechanism.

Lease Transfer

The lease must be transferred to you on terms that are acceptable, which is especially important if the business relies on its location to generate revenue.

Due Diligence

Give yourself enough time to inspect the company's books and records, and conduct a thorough review of the business. Usually 20 business days is adequate.

Training

Each business dictates how much time you need for postclosing training. Negotiate a period that makes sense for you. But if you think the seller should stay on for a year to train you, chances are you're buying the wrong business.

Step 6: Finance the Purchase

Banks have everyone fooled. From their ads, you'd think that their vaults are open and ready to lend money to budding entrepreneurs, but that's not reality.

There are only four ways to finance a small business purchase:

1. Pay all cash.
2. Borrow from family and friends.
3. Secure a government-financed loan.
4. Arrange seller financing.

The first three have downsides. The next section explains why.

Pay All Cash

Even if you can afford it, paying all cash doesn't make sense unless you get a massive price concession, or the deal is very small.

Borrow from Family and Friends

If you're going to count on family and friends, get them involved in the process and committed to exactly how much they will lend you. Their intentions may be sincere, but often they don't deliver. If you can't demonstrate that you have the resources, the seller or broker won't take you seriously.

Secure a Government-Financed Loan

The Small Business Administration (SBA) guarantees 75 percent of the loan a bank makes to you, and finances up to 80 percent of the deal. That kind of leverage is definitely attractive—but few get them. Both you and the business must qualify, and the standards, and the fees, are tough. In many cases, you'll be required to ante up substantial personal security, such as your house.

Arrange Seller Financing

I don't think you should ever buy a business without seller financing. What better way is there for the seller to validate that everything he or she has told you is true? If the seller won't finance part of the deal, don't agree until you get a substantial price concession, and you become familiar enough with the business to arrange alternate financing.

Interest rates can be negotiated and should be in line with the banks. In exchange for a longer term, agree to a higher rate. That may sound nuts, but you get more flexibility with a seller note that makes it worth it, and you can negotiate the following:

- A holiday from any payments for the first three to six months after closing
- The ability to make lump-sum principal payments throughout the term
- No lien against personal assets to secure the loan
- The right to payoff the loan early

If business is going well, think about paying off the whole note early. Mary Beth had $125,000 remaining on her note to the seller for two ladies' clothing stores. After two years, she called him up and offered to pay off the whole note immediately for $80,000. Later, she told me, laughing, that she could hear the seller starting his car when she made her offer.

Get Comfortable with Risk

Buying a business involves risk just like any entrepreneurial pursuit, and you must be willing to bet on yourself. There's no need to be reckless, but buying a business and providing a platform to accumulate wealth may force you to take some measures that you normally would not choose, and leveraging your personal assets may be part of the equation. Be prepared to take that step.

In my first significant business purchase, I leveraged myself up to the eyeballs, including every credit card I had available. But the $100,000 that I begged and borrowed for my first business grew into a $4.5 million company. Would I do it again? Yes! Why? Because I knew it was a good business that was perfectly suited to my skills.

Step 7: Do Your Own Due Diligence

In this stage, you will have access to all of the company's books and records. It's also the last step when you can back out of the deal legally without any obligations to the seller, and not forfeit any deposits. The due diligence clause in the contract must clearly state that you can retract your offer "at your sole and absolute discretion, for any reason whatsoever" and get the immediate return of any deposit with no further obligation to the seller. Make sure your attorney drafts "bulletproof" language on this point.

Allow yourself enough time to complete this phase, and don't restrict yourself to just the financials. Be wary of any seller or intermediary who pushes for a very limited period.

You must thoroughly investigate the financials, the assets, the competition, customers, employees, sales and marketing strategy, the systems in place, all contracts, the suppliers, and legal and corporate issues. Everything you need to do in these categories adds up to a 200-point checklist that you can find in the chapter, "Due Diligence," in my book, *The Art of Buying a Business*. Here are just a few:

- Have your attorney review all legal issues and liabilities, and verify any copyrights, trademarks, and patents.
- Instruct a CPA experienced with the industry to assemble a checklist of all financial documents, double check bank and financial statements, and perform a mini audit.
- Learn how the company generates its sales.
- Who are the customers, and will they continue to buy from you?
- Review all contracts, and, if there are any major clients representing more than 10 percent of the business, either meet with them before closing, or have a provision in the contract to protect you in case you lose them after you take over.
- Who are the competitors? How much of a threat are they?
- Hire an industry consultant to appraise equipment and estimate replacement costs.
- Are the systems adequate? If not, at what cost can they be replaced and/or implemented?

Dealing with Problems

Chances are you'll find some problems, but don't run to the seller over every little every issue. Build your case and wait. Every business has secrets and problems. Separate minor issues from the real catastrophes. When too many add up, you may need to renegotiate the deal.

STEP 8: CLOSE THE DEAL

The whole deal can get bogged down in the details by the time you compete your due diligence and the actual closing transpires. The amount of paperwork involved in the deal still blows my mind. I was at a closing last year that involved an SBA-backed loan, and I think there was over a foot-high pile of paper for the buyer to sign.

Get familiar with the paperwork. Your attorney will play a very important role in getting all of the documents together.

Lease Assignments

This document provides written consent from the landlord that he will assign the lease to you. The landlord may also want to see your résumé and financial statement. Landlords usually don't move too quickly on these documents, so be very specific about your targeted closing date. In deals where a seller remains on the lease as a guarantor for the remainder of the term, you may be expected to provide indemnification. Finally, be prepared for miscellaneous fees (landlord's out-of-pocket expenses, attorney fees, and office time).

Promissory Note

This is your personal guarantee to repay the debt to the lender. There is no need for you to pledge any personal assets or security if there is a note to the seller.

Other provisions include the right to:

- Pay off the entire amount at any time without penalty.
- Twice a year, make a lump-sum payment toward the principal, without penalty.
- Begin payments 30 to 180 days after the closing date.
- Negotiate, without interest, the first three to six months, to pay the principal payment only.
- "Set off" for any liabilities that may arise after the closing (e.g., the seller fails to pay a utility bill).

Lien Search and Filings

These documents provide proof that all assets the seller is delivering to you are free and clear. If the seller is holding a note on the sale, they may then file new liens against the assets as security to your loan.

Purchase Price Allocation

Have your accountant put the proposed purchase price allocation document together and negotiate directly with the seller's accountant. There are tax consequences for both buyer and seller that conflict with one another.

Transfer Taxes—Bulk Sales Taxes

You may be obligated to pay certain taxes and fees on the assets you acquire. On vehicles, or "rolling stock," there can be title fees, licenses, and taxes based on current value. Check with your attorney and accountant. These taxes vary from state to state.

I was involved in the sale of a large moving business, where the lender's attorney "forgot" to include these costs on the closing statement. The day of closing—in fact, 90 minutes before—he nonchalantly advised the buyer that he would have to come up with $810,000 more cash at closing. I told the bank they had to loan the buyer the additional money with very favorable terms, or lose the deal and be liable for the costs incurred by the buyer to rescind the offer, plus pain and suffering. Within three minutes, the bank's senior vice president was on the phone negotiating. You don't get this type of response in all deals, but a multimillion dollar deal was at stake. The lesson here is this: know the financial and contractual obligations involved before closing.

Your Next Step: Take the Ball and Run with It

Completing the information in this chapter is a lot like being the rookie quarterback who's just joined the pros. You arrive in the big leagues and everything—the uniform, the players, the fans, the coaches, and the entire playbook—is new. You spend each and every day learning new plays, watching videos, working with the coaches, studying the opposition, and practicing for hours. Then, it's showtime.! Are you nervous? Of course. Are you ready? Absolutely.! It takes a few plays to get over the jitters, but each day gets easier because you've prepared yourself and followed the right steps.

It's like that with buying a business: You prepared. You did your research. You studied the business. Now, it's time to close on the deal. As your coach, I say: "go get 'em! You're ready!" Whatever nerves or anxiety you may be feeling is strictly your eagerness to get the game—the business—going. Close the deal and you'll never look back. Never!

For More Information

For overall information, consult www.Bizquest.com.

On buying a business, consult www.BizBuySell.com and www. BusinessesForSale.com, which include listings in the United States and overseas.

For financial analysis and marketing research, visit www.BizMiner.com.

For government-financed loans, visit the Small Business Administration web site, www.sba.gov.

For brokers, consult www.brokerpages.com and the International Business Brokers Association (www.ibba.org).

V

Own Property:
The Real Estate Path
to Wealth

13

WHY YOU SHOULD INVEST
IN REAL ESTATE
by
Gary W. Eldred, PhD

To achieve financial freedom, and to enjoy a worry-free retirement that provides a prosperous quality of life, no investment outperforms real estate. Among the most popular asset classes, residential rental properties have offered the greatest returns for the least risks. "But those results lie in the past," you might say, "What about the future?" Good question, but my answer remains the same—with this caveat.

In the past, relative to stocks and bonds, most residential properties were severely undervalued. That value difference still favors real estate, but it's no longer a slam dunk. Buying property today requires more education and more market knowledge than you had to have during the great bull market in the first half of this decade.

Baby boomers scrambling to fund their retirements, pension funds racing to accumulate assets to fund their future liabilities, and the already affluent searching for ways to enlarge their wealth are bidding up the prices of all types of investments. The Dow Jones Industrial Average Stock Index now sits near its record highs, yields on long-term government bonds are fluctuating around 4.75 percent, not far from their 40-year highs, and the median price of a single-family house now sits above $225,000—more than twice the amount recorded 10 years ago.

There's no doubt: Today's investors (in all asset classes) face times more challenging than any period since at least the 1930s. In most instances, earlier investors have already picked the low-hanging fruit. Yet the stomach is growling louder.

CHALLENGE DOESN'T MEAN IMPOSSIBLE

Since the late 1990s, sharp increases in property prices, along with a corresponding relative decline in cash flows and rental yields, have led the major media to persistently babble about real estate "bubbles." Taking a cue from these misguided journalistic missives, many people now believe that real estate is no longer a good investment. But, if you expect a secular fall in property prices, don't hold your breath. Ever since the 1940s, such failed forecasts have periodically littered the economic landscape. Do not err by focusing on the low prices you missed in the past. Realize that 10 years from today—just as in every previous decade—today's property prices will seem low.

So, without a doubt, your efforts to build wealth should include residential rental properties. Although every type of asset class offers some promise, when viewed in total, the benefits of rental properties are tough to beat. When you invest in property, you can gain in 10 ways:

1. A competitive flow of income.
2. Leveraged returns.
3. Wealth from amortization.
4. Wealth from inflation.
5. Wealth from appreciation.
6. Strategic management.
7. Instant equity.
8. Optimal liquidity.
9. Income tax advantages.
10. Portfolio diversification.

No other investment can match such an extensive list of benefits.

A Competitive Flow of Income

When I first began buying rental houses and apartment buildings, I could easily find properties that offered net unleveraged rental yields of 10 percent to 16 percent. Net unleveraged rental yields refer to rent collections, less all cash expenses and mortgage financing. Calculate by dividing the price of the property into its net income (e.g., $10,000/$100,000 = 10% yield). In some areas of the country, such as the Midwest, you can still achieve such favorable results; more typically, today's rental properties yield 4 to 8 percent at the time of purchase. Relative to the past, 4 to 8 percent doesn't seem great, but relative to stocks and bonds, properties win hands down. (Remember, at this point, we're talking about income, not asset appreciation.)

Rental Properties versus Stocks   At present, the annual dividend (income) yield on the S&P 500 stock index falls below 1.8 percent, and less than 0.40 percent for NASDAQ stocks. The Dow-Jones (DJIA) is somewhat higher, at around 2.20 percent. If you follow the advice that says you must diversify across a broad variety of stocks, you might achieve a yearly income of $15,000 to $20,000 (1.5 to 2 percent average yield) from a stock portfolio valued at $1 million. In contrast, a million dollars in property value would return a rental income (net of operating expenses) of $40,000 to $80,000 a year.

Accumulate a million dollars in stocks and, to survive above the poverty level, you'll need to eat your nest egg (what financial planners call your withdrawal rate). But accumulate a million dollars in property and, to live an average-to-above-average lifestyle, you'll never need to eat your nest egg. Your net worth doesn't diminish—it will continue to increase.

Bonds versus Property   Currently, long-term investment grade bonds yield about 5.0 percent to 6.0 percent. Without taking on much default risk, that means you could count on receiving $50,000 to $60,000 a year from bonds for each $1 million you invest. Bonds deliver income returns that approach the level of income offered by high-quality rental properties. Also, compared with a fully diversified portfolio of stocks, bonds clearly rank superior, but here's the rub: your bond income will not increase as the result of inflation or economic growth and, as consumer prices go up, the buying power of your bond income will continuously erode. In terms of purchasing power, $60,000 of income today will equal $40,000 after just 10 years. In contrast, over time, both stock dividends and property rents tend to climb each year to higher levels.

The Verdict on Income   So what's the verdict? Stock income increases over time, but the puny yield produces too little income. Bonds return a better yield than stocks, but fail to offer the possibility of growth. Worse, in an inflationary economy, the real value of bond income declines. History indicates that you will achieve a competitive yield, growth, and protection against inflation with rental property.

Leveraged Returns

The previous discussion assumes you own your stocks, bonds, or property free and clear of debt (i.e., unleveraged). Nearly all financial advisors agree that investors should not borrow (and, in most cases, cannot borrow wisely) to acquire and/or finance stocks or bonds, because borrowing costs too much and poses too much risk.

Investors, however, can and do safely use debt to finance rental properties. To illustrate, let's do the math on a leveraged property acquisition.

Positive Leverage Boosts Cash Yields   You find a duplex priced at $200,000 that yields 7.5 percent. Instead of paying all cash, you acquire this property with a $160,000 mortgage, 6 percent, 30-year payoff (amortization). You put up $40,000 (i.e., your out-of-pocket cash) as a down payment. By leveraging your purchase, you boost your annual income yield from 7.5 percent to 8.44 percent. Here's the math:

Net income (.075 × $200,000)	$15,000
Annual debt service ($160,000 @ 6%, 30 years)	$11,624
Cash flow less debt service	$3,376
Leveraged return from cash flow (R) =	Cash flow/Cash invested
R =	$3,376/$40,000
R =	0.0844 or 8.44%

At first glance, you see that the *amount* of your available yearly income fell because you must pay your lender, but the yield on your cash investment climbed.

This simple example illustrates the method you can use to calculate leveraged returns from income. Depending on the property and terms of financing, your numbers can vary. In practice, investors often negotiate property price and terms of financing to meet some targeted "cash-on-cash" return objective. If they can't get the numbers they want, they search elsewhere (other properties, other cities). Most investors rely on leverage (OPM—Other People's Money) to enhance their annual yields from income.

Do Lower (or Negative) Cash Yields Make Sense?   In today's competitive marketplace, many investors accept leveraged yields from annual cash flow that actually falls below unleveraged yields, and in some areas, financing a property can even create negative cash flows.

To illustrate, let's assume that our $200,000 duplex yields a 5 percent unleveraged rather than a 7.5 percent unleveraged return. Here are the new numbers:

Net income (.05 × $200,000)	$10,000
Debt service ($160,000, 6%, 30 years)	$11,264
Cash flow less debt service	($−1,264)
Leveraged yield from income (R) =	−1,264/$40,000
R =	−3.16%

Does it make sense to buy and finance a rental property that produces these kinds of adverse numbers? Maybe.

Remember, to accurately evaluate any type of investment, compute *total* expected returns. Income contributes an important role, but also count other members of the cast.

How rapidly do you expect rents to climb? Can you boost net rental income through better management of the property? Can you convert the property to a more profitable use (e.g., rental apartments to condominiums)? How much will amortization (mortgage paydown), appreciation, and inflation add to your gains? How much tax shelter does the property provide?

When I started my career in real estate, investors applied this buying rule: "Pay for the present, get the future for free." If we couldn't get a property to yield a leveraged cash-on-cash return of 15 percent to 30 percent (depending on the quality of the property and its tenants), we passed on the deal. We expected large additional returns from the other sources just cited, but we considered those gains "gravy." We only paid for the "meat and potatoes" (current income).

Unfortunately, those glorious days no longer exist. Today, you may have to pay for the future. But given the generous future rewards you can expect—especially when contrasted to the relatively poor yields for stocks and bonds—even currently negative cash flows can make sense when the other sources of property gains listed earlier look good.

Wealth from Amortization

When investors think property, they generally want positive cash flow *and* appreciation, and over time, most rental properties fulfill these wants.

But what if a leveraged property never yields positive cash flows? Surprisingly, leveraged rental properties can provide a relatively attractive return, even without positive cash flows or price increases.

Say that after 20 years of ownership, your rent collections cover operating expenses, pay off the property's mortgage balance of $160,000, and give you a net *annual income* yield of zero. At the end of year 20, you sell this property for $200,000, your original purchase price, but by growing your down payment of $40,000 into free and clear property ownership 20 years later, you received a return on your investment of nearly 8.5 percent.

If your down payment was $20,000 (10 percent) and your rent collections paid off your mortgage balance in 20 years, your $200,000 purchase/sales price would bring you a return slightly over 12 percent.

Wealth from Inflation

A January 2006, article in *Money* magazine reported that since 1950, housing had appreciated at an average rate of 4.5 percent a year, and, after inflation, had generated quite lousy returns—about 1.6 percent a year. *Money* concluded that this proved housing yielded poor returns relative to stocks, essentially giving readers the advice: "if you want a great return on your investments, avoid property, buy stocks."(A similarly inept article, "Stocks vs. Real Estate" appeared in the May 2007 issue of *Money*.)

Never Trust a Journalist with Numbers   Never trust a child with a loaded gun, and never trust a journalist to interpret numbers. The rate of return figures and conclusions that *Money* reported mislead more than enlighten; quite significantly, *Money* omits the returns that property owners receive from rental income, tax shelter, and other sources. You cannot meaningfully compare the relative merits of alternative investments until you accurately account for the total risk-adjusted returns that each investment provides, or is reasonably expected to provide. But *Money* also errs for another important reason.

Leverage   Leverage multiplies the reported 1.6 percent inflation-adjusted real estate ROI. If investors paid 100 percent cash for their rental properties, the appreciation figure that *Money* calculated might prove correct. However, because nearly all property investors employ leverage, this calculation falls woefully short, in both method and result.

Let's return to our $200,000 property purchase. Say you sell this property after 10 years of ownership. At purchase, you invested a $40,000 down payment and financed $160,000 at 6 percent over a 30-year term. When you sell in year 10, you still owe a mortgage balance of $129,200. At *Money's* reported historical average annual price gain of 4.5 percent, your sales price equals $310,600. You pocket $181,400 ($310,600 less $129,200). During this period, inflation averaged 2.9 percent (4.5 − 1.6 = 2.9%), which means that you multiplied your $40,000 original cash investment by 353 percent. Yet, during the previous 10 years, inflation increased by merely 33 percent (2.9 percent compounded annually).

To match inflation, your original $40,000 would have to have grown to just $53,237, but, in fact, as measured by inflation-adjusted dollars, your $40,000 grew to $136,300 ($181,400 discounted over 10 years at the historical annual inflation rate of 2.9 percent). You can easily see from these figures that inflation-induced price increases greatly enhance the real wealth of investors who own property.

Inflationary Gains: Property versus Stocks   Over the longer term, U.S. inflation has averaged about 3 percent a year, although sometimes the country goes through extended periods of much higher inflation. One such period lasted from the mid-1960s until the early 1980s, when the Consumer Price Index (CPI) jumped more than threefold, from 95.4, in 1966, to 289.1, in 1982.

Between 1966 and 1982, the median price of a home escalated from $21,000 to $70,000. As measured by the Dow stock index (DJIA), equities not only failed to keep up with the CPI, they actually fell in *nominal* value. In 1966, the Dow hit 1,000. By January 1982, it registered a mere 875.

Will history repeat? No one knows. To guard against the risk of inflation, experience shows that no asset protects purchasing power as well as property, especially leveraged rental property. Even better, investment analysis demonstrates that leveraged property investors don't merely tread water during inflation; to their good fortune, their *real wealth* multiplies many times over.

To see the relative investment performance of property and stocks during this high inflationary period, look at Exhibits 13.1 and 13.2.

Wealth from Appreciation

Inflationary increases in the prices of materials and labor push up the costs of construction, and therefore the prices of properties. However, most properties also *appreciate* in value because demand presses against a constrained supply.

If you invest in properties that will benefit from the growth in jobs, incomes, and population, your properties will likely go up in value much faster than the long-term, average price increases of 4.5 percent a year. During the first half of this decade, such hot spots included Phoenix, Las Vegas, and

Exhibit 13.1   High Inflation? Stocks Lose, Property Gains

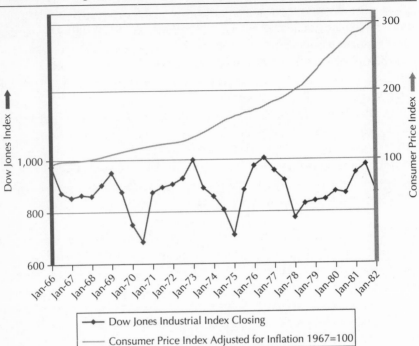

Miami. Between 1980 and 2005, San Francisco properties averaged price gains of nearly 8.0 percent annually. Over that 25-year period, San Francisco rentals returned relatively low yields from income during the early years of property ownership, but the outstanding jumps in equity that resulted from appreciation more than made up for those weak (and in many cases, negative) cash flows. Of course, over time, the long-term owners of rentals in San Francisco—as in other low-yield areas—were able to double and triple the original rents they collected when they first bought their properties.

Use the Real Estate Wealth Calculator at www.trumpuniversity.com/wealthbuilding101 to see three ways that real estate investments build wealth.

Income or Appreciation?   Should you trade off low, or even negative, income for a higher expected rate of appreciation?

As a *general* rule, housing markets today offer one of three choices:

1.   If you want to emphasize strong cash flows, you will search for properties located in geographic areas of slow, no, or even negative growth.

Exhibit 13.2   Median Price of Homes Sold in the United States, 1966–1982

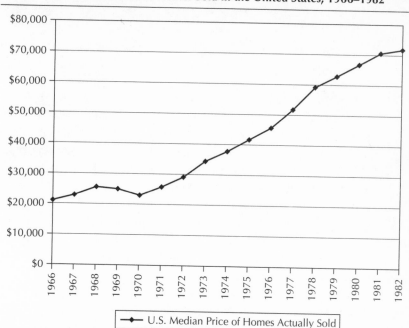

For example, in many so-called Rust Belt cities, rental properties earn unleveraged income yields of 8 percent to 16 percent a year. Great cash flows, but most investors expect these high-yield properties to appreciate slowly (or not at all).

2. If you want to gain the extraordinary wealth-building power of leveraged price appreciation, you might choose to buy in San Francisco, New York City, Boston, or other popular high-priced areas where buyers expect property prices to appreciate (over the long run) at rates substantially higher than the national average. Unfortunately, buyers in high-priced areas now must accept income yields of just 4 percent to 5 percent, and sometimes less. When financed with 80 percent loan-to-value mortgages, such properties can produce negative cash flows of $1,000 a month (or more —depending on the specific purchase price and terms of financing). Because of these large negative cash flows, relatively few beginning property investors can grab hold of this rung of the property ladder. They do not earn enough from their jobs to feed these 16-foot alligators. Many investors who can

afford to, won't, fearing that future price gains in high-priced, low-yielding areas might fall short of past experience. As a result, they believe these properties present too much risk.

3. If you can't afford, or don't want to, invest where you live—due to negative cash flows, or a stagnant or declining job base, you might consider a third type of property market, which represents emerging areas of growth—the optimal possibility. In these areas, you can find newly built properties that sell for less than $125 per square foot.[1] In addition, such properties tend to offer reasonable cash flows *and* high potential for future price increases. Many housing forecasters place Charlotte and Dallas into this "optimal" category. We revisit this emerging growth investment alternative in Chapter 14.

Strategic Management

In the eyes of many potential investors, owning rental properties entails too much hassle. "I'd never invest in property," some say. "Who wants to get called out at 2 A.M. to fix a stopped-up toilet?"

No doubt, if you self-manage real estate, you will put in time and effort, but unless you're a glutton for punishment, you will set up systems and trade persons to maintain and repair your properties. Self-management need not create an undue burden. In my early years, I self-managed dozens of my low- to moderate-income rentals. Yet, at the same time, I held a full-time university faculty position and also enrolled full-time in a rigorous PhD program in business.

To focus on negatives such as cleaning toilets, mowing lawns, or cajoling wayward tenants to pay their rent misses the more significant point: Property management offers a lucrative opportunity to craft a market strategy for your properties. Rather than a burden, self-management presents a blessing. As you will see in Chapter 14, self-management jumpstarts profits through entrepreneurial vision and execution.

Think Like an Entrepreneur

As an entrepreneurial owner, you figure out how to maximize your net income by tailoring your property's features and benefits to match the intense, unsatisfied needs and wants of a specific market segment of tenants.

Yes, you can steer clear of property management if you choose to, by delegating operational duties to a property management firm (or personal employee). Keep in mind, though, in our society, entrepreneurs earn the largest rewards—a bounty that lies out of reach for those less involved people who invest passively.

Instant Equity

If you buy publicly traded stocks or bonds, you will pay the current market value for these investments. You may enjoy price increases over time, but you will not immediately advance your current wealth. Not true for real estate. You can buy property for less than its market value. Common reasons that prompt sellers to discount their prices include:

- Financial distress
- Need for quick cash to pursue other opportunities
- Ignorance of the current market
- No eye for entrepreneurial transformation
- Unskilled sales/promotion efforts
- Desire for quick sale, minimum effort
- Desire to avoid paying a real estate commission

Recently, I bought a rental house for $150,000, but the mortgage loan appraiser placed this property's market value at $180,000 to $200,000. The seller lived out of town and had relied on an incompetent real estate agent for advice.

Such deals don't come along every day. Periodically, though, you will find (or negotiate) bargain prices that will increase your equity—and net worth—instantly.

Optimal Liquidity

Most investment advisors critique property because (they say) it lacks liquidity. According to this widely held view, if you want to cash out your real estate equity, you may wait months before you can get the property sold. In contrast, you can cash out stocks (or bonds) on a moment's notice.

Certainly, if you need cash to pay your bills, don't invest that money in property. Place it in a checking or money market account. But you want to lock up your piggy bank (that's why the government severely restricts early withdrawals from 401(k), 403(b), and IRA balances). Easy withdrawal means too many would-be investors squander their cash savings on exotic vacations, power boats, and new SUVs.

Fortunately, a so-called disadvantage of property—illiquidity—prevents impulse spending for expensive toys and extravagances. This fact works to your wealth-building benefit.

Nevertheless, you can you can manage the illiquidity issue in three ways:

1. Arrange a property equity credit line.
2. Arrange a cash-out refinance.
3. Sell the property quickly via an auction.

If you truly must convert property equity into quick cash, you need not wait months to do so.

Income Tax Advantages

Although it seems odd to use the words "tax" and "advantage" within the same phrase, the Internal Revenue Services (IRS) offers property owners a unique set of benefits, including:

- Not all of your net rental income is subject to income taxes. The tax code permits you to offset income with a deduction for depreciation.
- You can grow your portfolio of properties through Section 1031 exchanges and never pay income tax on accumulated gains.
- You can sell your personal residence and escape income taxes on the first $250,000 of gain ($500,000 if you're married).
- For some types of properties and property improvements, the IRS grants tax credits that reduce income taxes.
- If you pull gains out of a property via a cash-out refinance or equity credit line, that money comes to you tax free.

Admittedly, the IRS weaves each of these tax benefits within a web of rules and regulations that go beyond the space available here. (For more detailed treatment, see Chapter 14 in my book, *Investing in Real Estate*, fifth edition, John Wiley & Sons, 2006). Dollar-for-dollar, federal law permits property owners to pay less tax than investors who trade stocks or bonds. As an astute wealth builder, always evaluate and compare the after-tax returns of alternative investments.

Portfolio Diversification

As you can tell from this chapter, I prefer real estate to any other investment. I believe experience as well as reasonable forecasts affirm the favorable risk/ reward nature of this asset class.

Nevertheless, I also own stocks, bonds, intellectual property, CDs, and money market accounts. Even investors who love property as much as I do should diversify their wealth among a variety of investments. You should, too. If stocks better fit your personal investment criteria, then at least add some real estate to your holdings. Your property investments will counterbalance the cyclical, secular, and purchasing power risks that stocks force you to endure. But don't fall for the 5 percent to 10 percent real estate allocation favored by the many financial planners who serve as lapdogs for Wall Street.

Over the long run, stock indexes may climb. Yet, contrary to Wall Street dogma, stock prices can stay down for decades (even longer on an inflation-adjusted basis). Witness the periods 1907–1921, 1929–1953, and 1966–1982.[2] The time required for stocks to gain in value may outlast the years of your retirement.

No matter what asset class you (or your advisors) like best, never place more than 70 percent of your wealth into one asset basket.[3] A mix of asset classes may not enhance returns, but it does reduce risks. After you build your net worth, spread that wealth among differing investments.

14

Build Income
and Wealth with
Residential Properties
by
Gary W. Eldred, PhD

You've undoubtedly heard—and may actually believe—the cautionary advice, "The higher the potential rewards, the greater the risks." Now, here's the good news. To achieve their outsized returns, property investors need not take on outsized risks.

Currently, 30-year U.S. Treasury bonds yield less than 5.0 percent per year. To the capital markets, U.S. bonds present no risk of default. Now compare those Treasury bond yields to the yields on bonds backed by 30-year residential mortgages—about 5.75 percent to 6.0 percent. In other words, the capital markets say that mortgage bonds secured by the houses owned by you, me, and our neighbors, carry a risk just slightly above that of the U.S. government.

The capital markets readily open their vaults for homeowners and property investors because lenders face little chance of losing money on long-term loans backed by property (and, of course, creditworthy borrowers). Only one in 100 of these types of mortgage loans end in foreclosure. Lenders like the low-risk nature of property loans.

In this chapter, I show you how to value, finance, and manage one- to four-unit residential rentals. In Chapter 15, I explain how even beginning investors are expanding their horizons with other promising types of properties and property-related assets and activities.

VOLATILITY: STOCKS UNDERPERFORM PROPERTY

During a 5, 10, or even 20-year period, stock prices have fallen in value by 25 percent to 40 percent or more—especially when measured by inflation-adjusted dollars—while residential property prices consistently trend upward without severe price declines along the way. Except for speculative fever or sharp spikes in local unemployment, housing markets rarely experience nerve-rattling downdrafts.

The national median price for single-family houses sets a new record high nearly every year (see Exhibit 14.1). Do you know of any other asset that scores such dependable year-after-year gains? I don't.

People (Not Property) Account for Most Investment Losses

Both the capital markets and experience testify to the low-risk nature of property investments, but you shouldn't naively interpret low risk to mean "no risk worth noticing." Tens of thousands of homebuyers and property investors (often speculators) have lost (and will continue to lose) vast sums of money in real estate.

Why? Because they fail to gain detailed knowledge about the markets where they are investing (demand and supply). They blindly assume that the near future will mirror the immediate past. They take on more mortgage debt (or accept higher interest rates) than they can realistically pay. They foolishly believe the infomercial gurus who preach "no cash, no credit, no problem." They fail to anticipate the maintenance and renovation dollars that must be invested to sustain and enhance a property's value. They fail to thoughtfully address the needs and wants of their tenants. They destructively

Exhibit 14.1 The Median Price of a Home

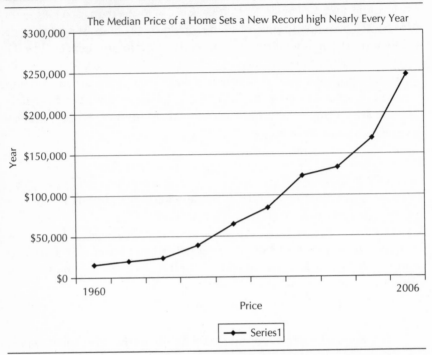

The Median Price of a Home Sets a New Record high Nearly Every Year

spend and borrow to support a conspicuous lifestyle they cannot legitimately afford.

In other words, people who suffer losses in property don't lose money because property investing entails high risk; they lose money because they fail to learn and apply the principles of property investment analysis and personal financial management.

EDUCATION PRECEDES SUCCESS

Please ignore the advice of anyone who claims that owning property itself will make you rich. Place the focus and responsibility for success on yourself. Repeat these words: "If I educate myself, if I discipline my spending and borrowing, if I learn the art and science of investing wisely, then through property I can build as much wealth as I want (or need)."

Acquire the knowledge that opens your mind and stimulates entrepreneurial insight, and then follow through with action.

What action? There are two proven strategies:

1. Pay less than the property is worth.
2. Maximize returns through strategic management.

Let's look at each in turn.

Pay Less Than the Property Is Worth

When you develop entrepreneurial insight, you see possibilities and probabilities that others miss. This skill plays a special role when you figure out how much a property is worth—and how to negotiate a bargain price. When I say buy at a "bargain price," did you think to yourself, "Pay less than market value"? If so, you are only partly right. Generally speaking, if you pay less than market value for a property, you have scored a good deal, but you can also pay less than a property is worth in other ways that rely on entrepreneurial talent. Here are several possibilities:

- *Find unused (or underutilized) space:* Have you seen ads for the California Closet Company? As this innovative firm (now copied by many imitators) has shown, you can increase (and even multiply) the space within a property without adding even one square foot of floor area. Through creative design, this company converts underused (or underutilized) closets, kitchens, garages, carports, attics, and so on to yield more benefits.

  Apply the same techniques as you value properties. Note the multiple ways that you can make existing space work more productively. Can you "rightsize" rooms, add cleverly designed shelves or cabinetry, or convert low-quality space (e.g., basements, attics, garages) into clean, dry, and convenient storage areas—or perhaps even additional living space?

  Remember, tenants choose properties that offer the greatest benefits for the amount of rent they're asked to pay. At very little cost, you can enhance the appeal and livability of most properties—when you envision possibilities.
- *Improve aesthetics:* Nearly everyone knows that aesthetically challenged properties sell at prices well below their GQ brethren. Find this ugly duckling. Pay market value. Improve it. You now own a property that's worth far more than the amounts that you invested.

When you evaluate a property, note in detail how it looks, feels, and sounds. How much would the property increase in worth if you:

1. Put in a skylight?
2. Installed noise-proof windows?
3. Created a view through use of flowers, shrubs, trees, and other landscaping?
4. Eliminated odors, unsightly views, and dark, dreary window coverings?
5. Modernized the baths and kitchens; or replaced worn or stained carpets?

Throughout my years of real estate investing, I have bought many properties at or near their current market value and, because I always buy with entrepreneurial insight, I see possibilities that others miss. With large doses of ideas and relatively small cash outlays for actual changes and improvements, these rentals (as well as some personal residences and commercial properties) were soon worth 20 percent to 40 percent more than I paid.

- *Reposition the property more profitably:* Along with property improvements—or even exclusive of any improvements whatsoever—you can often accelerate your profits by repositioning a property. As a rule, properties that target a specialized market segment earn higher profits than generic, run-of-the-mill rentals.

  For example, a property that appeals primarily to families with young children easily rents to this market segment at $1,000 a month. But through your market awareness, you learn that college graduate students who share accommodations typically pay $500 per bedroom. With three bedrooms in the property, this rental house could bring in $1,500 a month—if you shifted your market strategy.

  Different types of tenants value properties differently. I encourage you to develop the following three-step positioning strategy for your properties:

  1. Research your market.
  2. Figure out what types of tenants will pay the most for what you're offering (or could offer).
  3. Do what it takes to attract that market segment.

- *Buy at a bargain price:* Most real estate writers focus on one type of bargain—a property that you can buy below-market from that much sought-after, motivated seller. Unfortunately, the droves of investors who seek out these sellers greatly exceeds the few sellers who actually match this desperate profile.

Fortunately, entrepreneurs can pursue many other avenues. Cultivate your imagination. Systematically collect, study, and analyze market data. You will find that bargain-priced properties exist everywhere. Nurture your ability to recognize those nuggets of gold—even though they may be encrusted with mud.

- *Strengthen your borrower profile:* As you learned in Chapter 13, leverage can boost the returns you can earn from your properties, but you must persuade someone (a lender, the seller, your dad, etc.) to loan you the money. How do you accomplish this goal? Strengthen your borrower profile. Anyone who advances you cash will in some way question how well you satisfy these six Cs of loan underwriting:

1. *Credit:* Do you pay your bills on time, every time? Are you up to your eyeballs in debt or sitting comfortably debt free? What are your credit scores? (Review them at www.myfico.com and look for ways to lift them.)

2. *Cash invested:* How much of your own cash are you putting into the property? Are you seeking a loan-to-value ratio of 50 percent or 110 percent? Most lenders want you to put your own "skin in the game."

3. *Capacity:* Will your monthly income easily cover all of your monthly obligations and living expenses? Or are you stretched so thin that an unexpected trip to the dentist will put you into the red? (*Note:* If you're buying your first investment property, many lenders will not count your anticipated rent collections toward your qualifying income.)

4. *Cash reserves:* Do you save regularly? Have you accumulated a sizeable amount to keep you solvent during a period of job loss or illness? Can you cover your monthly mortgage payments on the new property even if it sits vacant for a month or two (which, with good management, should never occur)?

5. *Collateral:* Will the property appraise for more than your purchase price? What's the expected future for the neighborhood and city where it's located? How sound is your business plan and entrepreneurial vision for the property?

6. *Character:* Does your reputation support or contradict your plans and promises? In life's ups and downs, can people rely on you to honor your commitments, to do what you say you're going to do? Do people believe without doubt or reservation that they can (and should) trust you?

- To build wealth, maintain an impeccably strong borrower profile. A strong borrower profile opens doors locked shut to those with lesser credentials. "No cash, no credit" folks can frequently raise money to finance a property acquisition, but they will sacrifice a large part of their anticipated returns to higher loan costs, interest, and fees. They will lose many potential deals to people whose record affirms their character, their financial responsibility, their habits to spend below their means, and only borrow constructively—not destructively). Develop a strong borrower profile and lenders (as well as other investors) will compete to do business with you. A strong borrower profile will not only put more deals in front of you to consider, it will also give you the power to negotiate the most favorable deal/debt terms.

Maximize Returns through Strategic Management

Unlike day-to-day property management, strategic management creates a winning value proposition for your tenants and a high reward/low risk return on your investments of time, work, and money. To manage strategically and effectively, execute the following eight action steps:

1. *Before you buy, verify, verify, verify:* When you shop for a property, you will likely obtain information from sources (sellers, real estate agents, home inspectors, government officials, lawyers, fellow investors), and maybe even friends, relatives, and neighbors. You will seek information about property condition, rent levels, operating expenses, comp sales prices, zoning, building regulations, government rules and practices, neighborhood desirability, the features, quality, and rents of competing properties, and dozens of other facts, judgments, and opinions. To construct a base of knowledge, every investor must rely on data gathered from other people.

   But don't naively accept information. Check supposed facts through more than one source. Probe and explore the judgments and opinions that people share with you. Do they really know what they're talking about? What biases or conflicts of interest might color their views and advice? The price you pay, the market strategy you create, depends on facts and judgments. Verify, verify, verify. Does the information you possess really warrant your confidence?

2. *Craft a winning value proposition:* Your profit potential increases when you target specific market segments. Do you want your property to attract quiet college students, families with young children, Section 8 tenants, wheelchair-bound folks, or perhaps seniors who want an adult congregate living facility?

Provide your chosen tenant segment with the specialized features and benefits they want, and in exchange, they will reward you with higher rents, lower maintenance costs, and reduced turnover.

3. *Design a lease for your target market:* The terms and clauses within your lease should reinforce the competitive positioning of your property. Do not merely offer your tenants the same off-the-shelf, so-called standard lease form that your competitors mindlessly use. In addition to rent level, you could adapt nearly any clause in the lease to better appeal to a selected tenant segment. For example, you might:
   - Reduce (or increase) your upfront cash requirements.
   - Reduce (or increase) your credit qualifications.
   - Shorten (or lengthen) the duration of the lease.
   - Shorten (or lengthen) the payment periods (e.g., weekly for lower-income, annual at a discount for an affluent target market).
   - Permit (or prohibit) pets.
   - Include an option to renew at a guaranteed rental amount.
   - Include (or omit) appliances, furniture, and window coverings.
   - Include an option to buy the property with the lease.

   This list could continue, but you see the point. You not only tailor the features and amenities of the property to tenant preferences; but also craft a lease with their wants and needs in view.

4. *Attract top-flight tenants:* Now persuasively communicate the advantages of what you're offering. Don't just run a generic, look-alike, classified ad in the local newspapers. Write a compelling ad or flyer that extols the property's benefits and your outstanding value proposition. Then put the word out in a medium that offers the lowest cost per prospect reached.

   Find out where your target market currently lives, works, or shops. Investigate ways to stimulate word of mouth. Are there bulletin boards, newsletters, web sites, or housing offices/agencies where you could reach your desired audience? A sound market strategy incorporates a well-written and well-researched promotional campaign.

5. *Create a flawless move-in:* Now that you've attracted the perfect tenant for your property, begin your relationship on a positive note. Establish cordial relations. Avoid issuing stern orders as if you were an army drill sergeant. Explain house rules along with the reasons why the rules exist. In a friendly way, talk with the tenant about the behavior you expect. Also talk about your responsibilities (as imposed by law, the lease, or operating policies), and how you will diligently perform your landlord role.

Before you meet the tenant, verify that your make-ready has not overlooked any property defects such as a greasy stove, cracked windows, soiled carpets, missing keys, broken locks, or unsafe (or dysfunctional) wiring, electrical boxes, or wall outlets. In my experience, a flawless move-in sets the stage for a flawless tenancy.

6. *Retain top-flight tenants:* Tenant turnover (typically) costs you money. Even hotels prefer guests who stay a month to those who stay a couple of nights. To retain your quality tenants, adhere to these guidelines:

- *Keep tenants informed.* When something out of the ordinary (pest spraying, construction noise, utilities shut-off, etc.) is about to happen, notify your tenants beforehand. Tenants rightfully get upset when you unexpectedly disrupt their lives or invade their privacy.

- *Plan preventive maintenance.* Don't wait for problems to arise and then react. Breakdowns in the middle of the night add to your costs of repair. They create ill-will among tenants ("That's the third time this winter the furnace blower has stopped working."), and they may generate repair costs and replacements that otherwise would not have occurred (e.g., a broken step that results in injury and a lawsuit; a water leak that causes wood rot).

- *If you fail to care for your property, you can bet that your tenants will do likewise.* As your property deteriorates, your good tenants will leave. To fill your vacancies, you will have to accept tenants of lower quality who (more than likely) see your property as a temporary stopping point—not a home.

- *Enforce house rules.* Bad tenants drive out good tenants. If you misjudge the quality of a tenant at move-in, remedy that error immediately. Whether the problem(s) pertain to noise, pets, parking, or careless handling of trash or garbage, do not permit any tenant(s) to violate house rules. If you do, you'll end up with an apartment building full of rule-breakers.

7. *Even perfect tenants must pay their rent on time, every time:* Tenants who do not pay today will rarely pay tomorrow. If your tenants need financial assistance, refer them to a bank, their friends or relatives, a social services agency, or maybe a charity. Listen to my voice of experience: Forbearance foreordains problems.

If you wish to allow a nonpaying (or partial-paying) tenant to remain in the unit, do so for reasons of compassion, not business judgment. If at some point you must evict, adhere tightly to the lawful procedures of your city and state. If you fail to follow the law of eviction in every detail, a court may force you to refile and restart the legal process from the beginning. Even worse, if you violate some legislated (or court-dictated) tenant rights, the tenant may end up collecting a large sum from you.

8. *Persistently work to increase your rent revenues:* Even the perfect value proposition becomes less perfect—or even obsolete—over time. At least every six months, put on your Sherlock Holmes hat. Perform some detective work. Search through the "for rent" listings of classified ads, web sites, bulletin boards, and other potential sources. Focus on properties (more or less) similar to those you own.

Make phone calls. Visit units. Check out their condition, appeal, rent levels, application procedures, and lease terms. Then monitor your findings. How quickly are the units renting? What patterns or trends do you notice? From this market research, execute ways to profitably revise your value proposition.

What property features should you add (or upgrade)? Does the market justify a rent increase (or maybe even a decrease)? What market gaps (scarcity) or surpluses (lingering vacancies) are emerging? Should you reposition your properties to target a more profitable market segment?

What percent of all rental property owners systematically sleuth about their competitors? A majority? Or very few? You know the answer: Very few.

As a result, entrepreneuring in real estate offers many profitable opportunities.

In acquisitions, you can nearly always find ways to immediately enhance the rental revenues of a property, and in operations, you will enjoy higher occupancy rates, quality tenants, and longer-term residencies, for one very simple reason: You understand possibilities that your competitors never even knew existed. To help you determine what kind of real estate investment suits you download and complete Exhibit 14.2, The Real Estate Investor Self-Assessment at www.trumpuniversity.com/wealthbuilding101.

Downloadable Exhibit 14.2   Real Estate Investor Self-Assessment*

Question 1: Do you prefer to work on your own, or would you like to join with others to share equity financing, work, responsibilities, and decision making?

_____

_____

_____

_____

Question 2: How many hours per week are you willing to dedicate to looking for and buying properties?

_____

_____

_____

_____

Question 3: Will you make investment decisions on your own, or will you enlist the help of agents, lawyers, accountants, and others?

_____

_____

_____

_____

Question 4: What types of handyman talents do you have? Do you enjoy this type of work? How many hours per week are you willing to dedicate to repairing or improving your properties?

_____

_____

_____

_____

Question 5: What types of people would you like to attract as tenants? Will you manage your properties by yourself, or will you hire a property manager?

_____

_____

_____

_____

Question 6: What types of real estate would give you the greatest sense of personal achievement, pride of accomplishment, and ownership?

_____

_____

_____

_____

Question 7: How might your talents and inclinations constrain your choices of neighborhoods or properties? Are you willing to invest in any neighborhood, regardless of its condition? Are there any types of properties that you will avoid?

_____

_____

_____

_____

Note: A blank version of this exhibit can be downloaded from www.trumpuniversity.com/ wealth building101 for your personal use.

15

EXPAND YOUR PROPERTY
PORTFOLIO
by
Gary W. Eldred, PhD

R eal estate investors are expanding their horizons. For reasons of necessity, diversification, and, often, larger expected returns, many investors should consider exploring other types of property or property-related assets. Small residential rental properties located within their local area still remain a powerful way for investors who choose real estate investing to build wealth and create financial freedom, you too, might want to evaluate and compare one or more of the following alternatives:

- Lower-priced areas (United States and the world)
- Emerging growth areas

Parts of this chapter have been abridged and adapted from Gary W. Eldred and Andrew McLean, Chapter 15, "New Trends and Developments," *Investing in Real Estate*, 5th ed. (Hoboken, NJ: John Wiley & Sons, 2006).

- Emerging retirement areas
- Commercial properties (office, retail)
- Self-storage
- Mobile home parks
- Zoning changes
- Property/Property-related stocks

Remember, when you think like an entrepreneur, you persistently bring new possibilities into view. Mull over some of the ideas you'll discover in this chapter. Do not let lack of knowledge and vision constrict your ability to profit with property. Although this brief review of possibilities can't tell you everything you need to know to succeed, I hope that through this discussion, I can excite and motivate you to learn more about the unlimited potential that real estate provides.[1]

Lower Priced Areas

If you live in San Diego or Boston, you've seen small residential properties priced with unleveraged income yields as low as 4 percent to 5 percent, but in the Midwest, Southwest, and South, you will find similar properties (except for location, of course) that yield 6, 8, 10, or maybe even 12 percent. Exhibit 15.1 shows several examples of recent listings.

Exhibit 15.1   Sample Listings for Small Apartment Buildings

Phoenix, Arizona		
Painted inside and out, ceramic tile throughout units, some new appliances, new mini blinds, some new toilets, doors, tubs, and sinks. Units in well-kept condition.	Status:	Active
	Price:	$234,000
	Bldg. Size:	7,896 SF
	Units:	4
	Cap Rate:	8.60%
	Primary Type:	Garden/Low-Rise
Austin, Texas		
Built in 1973. Faces 1902 hearthstone with a large, fenced grassy area in between. Seldom has a vacancy. All units remodeled in 2001.	Status:	Active
	Price:	$177,500
	Bldg. Size:	3,584 SF
	Units:	4
	Cap Rate:	10.29%
	Primary Type:	Fourplex

Rockwall, Texas

21% cash on cash. Very nice units in a park-like setting in the fastest-growing county (Rockwall) in the United States. Rockwall has a moratorium on new construction.

Status:	Active
Price:	$135,000
Bldg. Size:	2,586 SF
Units:	3
Cap Rate:	9.47%
Primary Type:	Garden/Low-Rise

Omaha, Nebraska

Mid-city brick units: 8 courtyard and 3 below grade. Three built-in garages. Boiler (owner pays heat and water). One-quarter acre.

Status:	Active
Price:	$330,000
Bldg. Size:	6,000 SF
Units:	11
Cap Rate:	30.00%
Primary Type:	Garden/Low-Rise

Roanoke, Virginia

Brick apartment building with balance of efficiency, 1-bedroom, and 2-bedroom apartments. Centrally heated with updated electrical and new roof.

Status:	Active
Price:	$258,000
Bldg. Size:	7,500 SF
Units:	10
Cap Rate:	9.3%
Primary Type:	Mid/High-Rise

Fort Myers, Florida

Updated duplex consists of two 2-bedroom, 2-bath units. Each unit is over 900 square feet. The exterior has been repainted and reroofed. Two parking spaces per unit.

Status:	Active
Price:	$118,000
Bldg. Size:	1,943 SF
Units:	2
Cap Rate:	8.7%
Primary Type:	Garden/Low-Rise

Tonawanda, New York

Nearly new apartment complex, thirteen years young, all 2-bedroom apartments. Separate utilities, central air conditioning. Laundry rooms and parking on site.

Status:	Active
Price:	$349,900
Bldg. Size:	8,305 SF
Units:	8
Cap Rate:	9.50%
Primary Type:	Garden/Low-Rise

Go to www.loopnet.com. Click on locales away from the East and West coasts. Troll through for sale listings. You'll find thousands of properties priced in the same range as those shown in Exhibit 15.1 (residential as well as offices, retail, mobile home parks, self-storage, industrial, etc.). Many of these properties sell for $100 per square foot (or less) and will produce positive cash flows with a down payment of 20 percent. Get away from the high-priced cities, and you can buy quads for $200,000 that generate rent collections of more than $1,500 a month.

When I lived in Dubai (UAE), a colleague owned four rental properties in France, another owned rentals in Alabama, another owned rental houses located in Perth—and none employed a property management firm. You can self-manage rental properties from anywhere in the world. Don't be afraid of long-distance property management. Here's the secret: Offer good value and select great tenants. Put a system in place to handle repairs, vacancies, emergencies, and you shouldn't encounter serious difficulties.

Tenant-Assisted Management

You may need local assistance. For intermittent vacancies and general property oversight, you should enlist the help of one of your longer-term tenants. In exchange, you can give that tenant discounted (or free) rent and a variety of upgrades for his or her living quarters.

Property Management Companies

As a general rule, I do not recommend using large residential property management companies, although other investors I know find them satisfactory. I don't think this type of firm will strive to give my properties the competitive advantage that I'm seeking because they are also working for dozens of my competitors. If self-management issues deter you from investing out of your area, then by all means employ a property management company. Just make sure the company follows your entrepreneurial strategy. Delegate, don't abdicate.

EMERGING GROWTH AREAS

Recently in San Francisco, I shared the speaker's platform with Richard Florida (author of *The Rise of the Creative Class*, New York: Basic Books, 2003) and Rich Karlgaard (publisher of *Forbes* magazine and author of *Life 2.0.*, New York: Crown, 2004). Neither claims expertise in real estate, but both offer real estate investors good points to ponder.

In different ways, Florida and Karlgaard have researched the areas of the United States, as well as specific cities, which will experience long-term profitable growth. They point out that today, people do not necessarily move to where the jobs are; rather jobs (at least the best-paying jobs) move to where the population that Richard Florida dubs the "creative class" want to live.

Implications for Potential Profits

As you evaluate areas for growth (appreciation), review socioeconomic statistics such as jobs, incomes, and household size. Notice the types of people moving into an area; the types of employment; and the restaurants, cafes, and bookstores that are opening. Discover what festivals, tournaments, outdoor activities, and sports events are gaining in size and recognition.

Is the area, whether a neighborhood, city, or rural outpost, attracting people who will serve as drawing cards for others? Seek areas that are developing cachet. Look for areas where increasing numbers of people say they would like to live. Such dreams encourage conversations and positive word-of-mouth. Such talk reinforces the decisions of those who decide to move. Many of us like to provoke at least a mild amount of envy from our friends, relatives, and acquaintances, and where we live, and where we are moving to, says a lot about us to those we know.

Right Place, Right Time

When I read Florida's discussion of the "creative class," I could see reflections of my own job moves. Throughout my career, I never accepted a job anywhere that I did not want to live. Those places (Vancouver, Palo Alto, Berkeley, Charlottesville, Williamsburg, Dubai), rank highly as creative class growth centers.

Yet, before reading this author's book, I thought of my location decisions as personal choices, not as "class" choices. It didn't occur to me that millions of other baby boomers would like to choose the same (or similar) locations—and thus push up property prices at an accelerated rate.

Apply my experience, as well as Florida's and Karlgaard's research and observations. Don't just personalize—generalize. What places do you like that have yet to hit their full stride? What cities do you hear others talking about? What locations have you read about in favorable articles? Identify "creative class" areas, and you have probably identified a promising area to invest.

Cash Flows and Emerging Growth Areas

As a rule, rental properties in emerging growth areas don't generate cash flows like a slot machine, but they certainly outperform established "creative class" areas such as Silicon Valley, Seattle, Boulder, and Washington, D.C. If you invest in Charlotte, for example, you can find appealing properties

Exhibit 15.2   Cash Flows Increase over Time

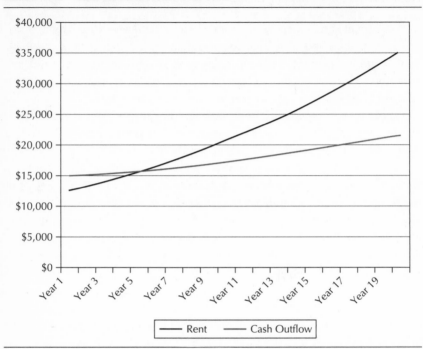

that in the first few years produce break-even (or slightly negative) cash flows, depending on the amount of down payment, interest rate, and term of amortization. But within three to five years, increasing rent collections should put you firmly into positive cash flow territory, as Exhibit 15.2 shows.

When you combine increasing income with the powerful wealth-building effects of leverage and tax shelters, emerging-area profits should yield long-term total returns of 12 percent to 15 percent a year, and possibly more. Many property investors now believe that emerging growth areas offer a package of investment attributes (low risk, growing income, above-average appreciation) that, overall, provides a solid investment choice.

EMERGING RETIREMENT/SECOND HOME AREAS

Between now and 2025, the number of persons in the United States age 60 or older will double. It is the largest age shift in U.S. history. Just as important, millions of these post-60 households rank among the wealthiest. Many other boomers are still seeking to build their wealth and incomes through property investment. Without a doubt, demand for retirement/second home property will remain strong from both retirees and baby boomer investors.

Combine this demographic age wave with increasing longevity, and you can see a continuing boom in prices for properties located in areas that become favored vacation/retirement spots. If you wish to invest for high appreciation, search out the towns, cities, and rural retreats that will be favored by this coming age wave. In fact, many property investors now look for areas that will gain from both creative class and age wave demographics.

Where to Invest

You can identify soon-to-be vacation/retirement meccas in the same way that you can identify emerging creative class locations. Talk with future retirees. What areas are achieving attention and increasing popularity? Personalize, then generalize. What locations seem attractive to you, your family, your friends, and your coworkers? Pick up a pile of books and magazines with titles relating to where to retire. Look for ideas, not answers. Whether you rely on information from publications or people you know, invest only in areas where your independent study reveals promise.

Income Investing

Many people who buy vacation retirement properties plan to rent them out part of the year and personally enjoy the property at other times. Although this strategy can work well, watch out for exaggerated estimates of rental revenues.

Demand for seasonal rentals varies according to weather (too much rain, too little snow), traffic and transportation issues (road construction, cost and availability of flights, etc.), and negative publicity (the SARS scare slashed travel to Toronto and Hong Kong). In addition, to manage vacation and seasonal rentals, vacation management companies charge 20 percent to 40 percent of gross rental receipts. For a full discussion of this investing strategy, see my book, *The Complete Guide to Second Homes for Vacations, Retirement, and Investment* (Hoboken, NJ: John Wiley & Sons, 2000).

COMMERCIAL PROPERTIES

Nearly everyone is familiar with investing in houses, condos, and apartments, but relatively few people realize that commercial properties also offer substantial promise. In today's real estate market, many commercial properties offer lower prices and higher income yields than houses, condominiums, and small apartment buildings. If you shop www.loopnet.com, you'll find thousands of office and retail properties priced at less than $500,000. Such properties often display unleveraged income yields of 5 percent to 8 percent.

Property Management

Depending on the type of property and the terms of your leases (see later discussion), you may not need a property management company, or a leasing agent.

Say you buy a medical office condominium that is leased to a doctor for a remaining term of five years. This doctor has three five-year renewal options. If she chooses not to relocate, you enjoy long-term, virtually carefree investment. The condo association maintains the building common areas, and the doctor accepts maintenance responsibility for the interior of her offices.

The Upsides and Downsides

One strong upside of commercial properties is that, in most, but not all, situations, your tenants operate businesses or professional practices. They establish themselves in a set location and, as a result, typically move infrequently. On the downside, when you do get a commercial vacancy, that space can remain vacant for months, and if you own a specialized property, or a property in an inferior location, a vacancy can last for years.

When you buy a commercial property with expiring leases on the near horizon, verify the marketability of the units (price and time on market). Do not naively assume that you or your leasing agent can quickly rent those vacancies.

Commercial Leases Create (or Destroy) Value

Generally tenants who rent residential units sign leases of one year or less. If a buyer doesn't like the previous property owner's lease, or tenants, he can write his own lease and operating policies and put them into practice within a short time.

With commercial properties, you probably face a different situation. Many commercial leases run for 3, 5, 10 years, or longer. Plus, commercial tenants often enjoy the right to renew for multiple periods (e.g., an original five-year lease with three- to five-year renewal options).

Just as important, commercial leases can differ greatly in their terms. Even various tenants who rent within the same office building or shopping center might have signed very different leases. That's because the terms of commercial leases depend on the market conditions when the lease is signed, and the relative negotiating powers of the tenant and the property owner. Tenants who signed office rentals in Silicon Valley in 2003 negotiated much sweeter deals than those tenants who signed at the peak of the tech boom of 1999–2000.

How Leases Differ

Lease terms determine your net income. Great leases keep your net income high, and leases with adverse terms drive your income down. Here are several examples:

- Who pays what? In commercial leases, property owners often shift some, or all, off the property's operating expenses to the tenant. In some leases—especially long-term, single tenant properties—the tenant pays for operating expenses, building repairs, and major replacements (e.g., roof, parking lot, an heating, ventiliation, and air conditioning system or HVAC).
- On what space does the tenant pay rents? Commercial tenants frequently pay rent per square foot, but the rentable square footage may exceed the tenant's private usable space. Some leases require tenants to pay rent for hallways, common areas, HVAC rooms, storage areas, public restrooms, and others. The lease may even specify the precise way the space is to be measured, which can add or subtract 5 percent, or more, to the quantity of rentable space.
- Are the rents inflation protected? If the property is leased to a tenant for 5, 10, 15 years, or longer, will your rent collections increase with inflation? When and by how much?
- Are the property owners entitled to percentage rents? Especially in retail, leases may require tenants to pay a base amount of rent plus a percentage of the tenant's business revenues which should be precisely defined; for example, must the tenant pay a percentage of their off-premises sales?

Read Each Lease Carefully

I don't want to make leases sound too complex. Some owners of small commercial properties write relatively simple, three- or four-page leases that involve month-to-month tenancies. However, unless you actually read through each existing lease, you won't know what pitfalls may be lurking within the fine print.

You don't want to buy a property only to learn that an undesirable tenant still has eight years to run on his lease at a rent level that is $6 per square foot below the market price. Or a small retail center with the idea of bringing in a Dollar General Store only to learn that an existing tenant had negotiated an exclusive "general merchandise" clause in its lease.

For more information, I recommend Thomas Mitchell's *The Commercial Lease Guide Book* (Macore International, 1992), and Janet Portman's and Fred Steingold's *How to Negotiate Leases for Your Small Business* (Nolo Press, San Francisco, 2005)

SELF-STORAGE

The self-storage industry is booming. Americans have become a population of pack rats. Our need for storage space grows larger every year. Although big players such as Shurgard attract most of the attention, smaller investors can also profit in this business. Exhibit 15.3 shows several sample listings from loopnet.com. You can see that self-storage can yield reasonably good cap rates (unleveraged income yield), often, you can earn even more if the site will

Exhibit 15.3 Sample Listings for Small Self-Storage Centers

Savannah, Tennessee	Status:	Active
A-1 Mini Storage consists of 79 units	Price:	$350,000
with a good unit mix. Situated on three	Bldg. Size:	14,340 SF
acres of land with room for expansion.	Cap Rate:	9.5%
	Primary Type:	Self/Mini-Storage Facility
Denison, Texas	Status:	Active
83 watertight mini-storage units on	Price:	$335,400
1.7 acres near Lake Texoma. Good	Bldg. Size:	9,575 SF
visibility, fenced with electronic gate.	Cap Rate:	9.30%
Construction 2003.	Primary Type:	Self/Mini-Storage Facility
Klamath Falls, Oregon	Status:	Active
Built to suit mini- and RV-storage	Price:	$150,000
facility in high-density mobile home	Bldg. Size:	5,200 SF
community and residential neighbor-	Cap Rate:	8.00%
hood. Cost includes 48 self-storage	Primary Type:	Self/Mini-Storage Facility
spaces.		

accommodate expansion. Alternatively, self-storage can provide a profitable way to hold land while you wait, say 3 to 10 years, to redevelop the site into a higher and better use (e.g., retail offices).

MOBILE HOME PARKS

You can invest in mobile home parks in two ways:

1. Own the set-up pads, provide utilities, and maintain the site; or
2. Own the pads and the mobile homes.

Exhibit 15.4 shows a sample of listings.

As with self-storage investments, you can hold mobile home parks for cash flow until the time is ripe to redevelop into a more profitable use. It's also common practice to delegate day-to-day management to a park tenant. Typically, park tenants are always looking for ways to make extra money.

Exhibit 15.4   Sample Listings for Small Mobile Home Parks

Sedgwick, Maine		
This new, seven-acre mobile home park is being offered for sale to settle the estate of the original developer, now deceased.	Status:	Active
	Price:	$195,000
	Bldg. Size:	N/Z
	Spaces:	20
	Cap Rate:	8.5%
	Primary Type:	Mobile Home/RV Community
Ridgecrest, California		
18 spaces and two houses will transfer with sale. All spaces have full hookups. Property is a turnkey operation with very low maintenance.	Status:	Active
	Price:	$221,000
	Bldg. Size:	1,111 SF
	Spaces:	18
	Cap Rate:	9.50%
	Primary Type:	Mobile Home/RV Community
Wilder, Idaho		
New terms! Seller may carry with $40,000 down. 12-space mobile home park with one park-owned mobile. On city services, paved street. Can assume loan.	Status:	Active
	Price:	$219,000
	Bldg. Size:	43,560 SF
	Spaces:	12
	Cap Rate:	9.30%
	Primary Type:	Mobile Home/RV Community

If you buy a park that includes mobile home rentals (rather than just the pads), value the park separately. Rental mobile homes generate strong cash flows, but they can wear out quickly. If you calculate their rental income to figure their worth, you will overpay. You can easily buy repossessed mobile homes for a fraction of their cost new. Value mobile homes as you would a used car.

PROFITABLE POSSIBILITIES WITH ZONING

As property investors struggle to boost their income yields, zoning and land-use opportunities are becoming more important. If you can add another floor to a rental house, sell off extra land as a buildable lot, or convert a house to an Adult Congregate Living Facility (ACLF), you can pocket thousands of dollars of found money (for more discussion of profit-making ideas, see my book, *Make Money with Fixer-Uppers and Renovations*, Hoboken, NJ: John Wiley & Sons, 2004).

Investigate whether you can enhance a property's current use and profitability within current zoning and regulatory rules. Sometimes the government changes a property's rules of use, and current property owners don't notice or don't investigate the maximum usage permitted. Alternatively, figure out a way to persuade planners and elected officials to grant your property (or area) a higher and better use.

PROPERTY AND PROPERTY-RELATED STOCKS

These past three chapters have repeatedly encouraged you to develop and nurture your abilities to think like an entrepreneur and open your mind to possibilities and probabilities that less thoughtful and enterprising folks miss. If you do, you can multiply your potential for profits while diminishing your risks. Through intelligence, effort, and entrepreneurial talent, you can almost guarantee yourself a winning outcome. Not everyone wants to think like an entrepreneur, or own investment property. If that's the case for you, consider buying shares of real estate investment trusts.

What Are Real Estate Investments Trusts?

Real estate investment trusts (REITs) are companies that own income-generating properties (or, in some cases, mortgages). Some REITs specialize in large apartment complexes, office buildings, shopping centers, self-storage facilities, or industrial properties. Other REITs own a mix of property types.

REITs provide a way for you to invest in property without taking on any of the managerial responsibilities (or enjoying any of the entrepreneurial opportunities) that direct ownership entails.

Where Can You Buy REIT Shares?

Many REITs trade publicly on the New York Stock Exchange. You can also buy mutual funds that own shares in a dozen REITs or more. As another possibility, you can invest in private REITs. Typically, shares in private REITs are sold by financial planners and many Wall Street stock brokerage firms. (*Caution*: Unlike the publicly traded REIT shares that you can buy/sell on the major stock exchanges, private REITs may not offer good liquidity. You may not be able to easily sell your shares.)

Benefits of REITs

Most people can't afford to buy a Manhattan office building, a 600-unit Dallas apartment complex, or a Miami regional mall. So REITs give you the opportunity to become part-owner of these and similar multimillion-dollar properties.

In addition, public REITs offer the same liquidity as other publicly traded stocks. REITs also provide their shareholders relatively high dividend yields compared to the yields of the S&P 500 or the Dow Jones average. Over time, as their owned properties increase in price (inflation and appreciation), REIT share prices also tend to increase. When in compliance with various requirements set by the Internal Revenue Service, REITs pay no income taxes on their net incomes.

Risks of Real Estate Investment Trusts

When trading as stocks, share prices can jump up and down according to the whims of the stock market and investor sentiments. REIT share prices exhibit far more volatility than the values of their underlying properties. Their share prices and dividends can fall if management fails to acquire and operate the properties profitably. Overall, though, for the past 30 or 40 years, REITs have delivered their shareholders quite favorable, risk-adjusted, total rates of return.

Homebuilders and Mortgage Companies

In addition to REITs, you can profit with real estate related investments when you own shares in homebuilders such as the publicly traded builders K&B, Toll Brothers, WCI, and D.R. Horton. You might also buy shares in financial institutions that deal heavily in mortgages. Countrywide, Fannie Mae, and Freddy Mac represent three possibilities.

Because homebuilding and mortgage lending run in major up and down cycles, the share prices of companies that operate in these businesses also swing up and down widely. As a result, if through your research you decide that a certain builder or lender shows great promise for long-term growth and profitability, a big cyclical downturn opens the door for you to earn big gains. Buy low (when negative feelings dominate). Sell high (when boom times come back).

Portfolio Diversification Revisited

The mainstream financial press often writes about asset allocation as if real estate represents a single category. As you now know, this simplistic approach badly misses the mark. Combine a variety of property and property-related investments described in this chapter, (different types of properties in different geographic areas, REITs), and you can achieve significant diversity yet remain within the general category of real estate.

You can even profit with property in many ways that I have not had space here to discuss (fix and flip, land banking, land development, triple net leases, low-income tax credits, discounted paper, and property tax lien/tax deeds.). So when a financial writer or financial advisor tells you that you should not hold more than 5 percent or 10 percent of your assets in real estate, laugh at him.

You want diversification and the highest risk-adjusted returns you can get. In today's marketplace of investments, to a much larger degree than most people realize, you can meet both of these objectives with real estate.

VI

Invest in Wall Street:
The Stock Market Path
to Wealth

16

GROW YOUR RETIREMENT
NEST EGG WITH STOCKS
AND BONDS
by
Philip A. Springer

With my father's guidance, I started investing in the stock market when I was 14 years old, using my earnings from delivering newspapers. The profitable proceeds from my first investment paid for three months in Europe when I was 20 years old. My second investment's "winnings" paid for a nice car. No wonder I liked the idea of buying shares of stock in a company and letting other people do the work to increase the value of my investment. I was hooked.

Easy, right? Not exactly.

As I've discovered over the subsequent decades, investing is hard work if you want to be successful over the long haul. It's easy to make a lot of money under the right conditions, but it's even easier to lose much more (and much faster, too) when the markets turn against you, if you're not prepared.

Yet investing for retirement (or any other long-term goal) isn't rocket science either. However, like life itself, investing can't be reduced to a few formulas. What works today might not work next year. Markets change; economic conditions change; companies change. But that's great because it means that there are many ways for you to make money and achieve your financial security. You don't need to be a genius. You just need to learn how to succeed.

At this stage of my life, fortunately, I've gone well beyond saving for a trip to Europe or a car. So, in this chapter, I want to share with you what I've learned over the years as an investment advisor for people who want to achieve and have financial security for their retirement.

As my father always stressed, "Knowledge is power." Dad didn't mean the power to control other people. He meant the power to control your own destiny, no matter what happens out there in the "real world." To him, that meant not necessarily academic education, but primarily learning what you need to do to achieve your goals. And investment success—by that I really mean achieving financial security—is open to anyone who works at it, regardless of how much "book learning" you have. In fact, one of the best investors I know got no further than the sixth grade. I've learned some good lessons from him.

START WITH TWO SMART STEPS

The first most important step for you to take, if you're not doing it yet, is very clear:

1. Save as much as you reasonably can. To reach financial independence in the future, be it at 65, 55, or 45, you need to live below your means now. Yes, it's that simple. Curb your spending—without being a nut about it. Save at least 10 percent of your annual income, and preferably 20 percent or more, depending on your current income, your age, and your future needs. Assuming that your investment portfolio appreciates 8 percent a year on average—a reasonable expectation—each $1,000 saved and invested this year will double in nine years, double again in 18 and double again in 27, to $8,000. That's the power of investment growth, compounding year after year.

The second most important step:

2. Recognize the importance of growing your wealth in more than one area. If you're an employee, take full advantage of whatever opportunities your company offers for saving and investment, such as a 401(k), 403(b), or other employer plan, where earnings will grow free of tax until you withdraw the money. In addition, if you're employed but have a part-time business, you can start and contribute to another retirement plan, too, such as a simplified employee pension (SEP) IRA, a SIMPLE-IRA, or a Self-Employed 401 (k).

Even if you have your own business, it's only good sense to set some money aside for long-term investment. True, entrepreneurs often have the best opportunities for wealth creation by putting their money into and growing their own businesses. Yet the risk of failure here can also be high, so it's wise to diversify your avenues for wealth building.

Don't make the all-too-common mistake, popularized in recent years, of thinking that your home is your best investment, and that it will pay for your retirement. Your home may well be your biggest asset, and it contributes a lot to your peace of mind. But just because the price you can get for it today or in the future may be much higher than you paid, it doesn't mean you've made a big profit. Reason: A home costs much more to buy and operate—out of pocket, year after year, aside from tax benefits—than most people realize because of mortgage interest, taxes, insurance, repairs, renovation, and so on. Plus, home prices don't always go up over time.

SEVEN SMART WAYS TO INVEST FOR RETIREMENT

I want to put you on the right path toward achieving a wealthy lifestyle in retirement (whenever that may be). For over 26 years, I've been helping people build a strong financial foundation for retirement. All too often, I've seen them make mental mistakes that lead to all sorts of financial fiascos. Here are my retirement rules for steering clear of disasters:

1. *Don't "play the market."* Investing for your financial security is serious business. In my view, the first and most important step to take is to adopt the right attitude. By that I mean how you view the world of investments and the financial markets.
2. *Learn to manage risk.* Recognize what can go wrong. Actively lower your risk exposure when necessary, but also get more aggressive when

market conditions turn very favorable, which means risk is low. Controlling risk—not trying to beat the market—should be your guiding objective.

3. *Control your emotions.* Investors who get into trouble typically become too enthusiastic when prices are rising and/or they panic when prices are sinking. Things are rarely as good as the blind optimists say, and almost never as bad as the professional pessimists would have you believe.

4. *Recognize that the investment markets themselves are not always rational.* They incorporate the knowledge and feelings of the world's investors on a daily basis, so they reflect the ongoing battle of those two all-too-human emotions, greed and fear.

5. *Pay close attention to the message of the markets themselves, and much less to the news headlines, market pundits, or TV talking heads.* How the markets react to external developments is much more important that the instant analysis of the "experts."

6. *Accept the fact that investing is more art than science, and that you'll often be wrong.* But try to learn from your inevitable mistakes so that you don't make the same ones over and over.

7. *Focus on the long term, not on daily fluctuations.* The longer your time horizon, the more likely it is that you'll stay calm and be right about an investment. The shorter your investment time period, the less likely you are to make and keep investment profits.

Now you have a good idea of how to approach the process of investing for retirement. As you actually invest, a key question you'll need to answer is whether to use individual stocks or bonds, or more diversified vehicles—that is, different types of mutual funds. Individual stocks offer greater potential reward than mutual funds, for instance, but also higher risk.

In general, I believe that most investors should use mutual funds entirely, or primarily, unless they have the interest, the time, and the developing expertise to research individual securities. Funds also provide the essential quality of diversification, which you're unlikely to achieve with fewer than a dozen or so stocks from different industries. In fact, even as a professional advisor, I've found over the years that it makes sense to use both individual issues and funds. This enables my clients and family to benefit from my expertise in certain parts of the financial markets, and to profit from the skills of others who are experts in other areas.

After you retire, you don't want to discover that you don't have enough resources to be comfortable. Determining how much money you'll need to retire is essential so that you can figure out how much you should set aside while you're working and help determine the types of investments you should make. Exhibit 16.1 is a worksheet that will help you determine how much you need to save each year to meet your retirement goals. Note that the assumptions you use can make a big difference in the outcome. Here are the relatively common assumptions I'm using:

- You'll retire at age 62 or later.
- Your goal is to provide enough income for a comfortable retirement, but not to build an estate.
- Your tax bracket in retirement will be about the same as when you were working.
- Your income and savings will rise with inflation until you retire.
- You want your spending to increase with inflation in retirement.
- Inflation will average 4 percent per year. *Note:* This is a conservative projection—inflation is now under 3 percent—that gives you an extra safety margin.

You'll need to supply certain other assumptions, such as when you'll retire, time spent in retirement, and a projected return on your investments. If you're in good health, my advice is to assume that you'll live until age 90.

I suggest that you do this worksheet several times, using different assumptions so you know how much leeway you have. Revisit this crucial question every year or so to make sure you're on track to meet a rich, worry-free retirement. To download your worksheet, visit www.trumpuniversity.com/wealthbuilding101. Now let's look at the investing process, beginning with stocks.

Downloadable Exhibit 16.1   Worksheet to Assure You Are Financially Able to Enjoy a Rich, Worry-Free Retirement*

Step 1: $_____
Your current annual income, before taxes.

Step 2: $_____
Annual income you'll need in retirement (in today's dollars). Use either an amount you estimate or 70 percent to 80 percent of your current income.

Step 3: $_____
Your annual Social Security benefits in today's dollars. You can obtain your "Personal Earnings and Benefit Estimate Statement" from Social Security (www.ssa.gov).

Step 4: $_____
Your estimated annual benefit from a fixed annual pension, if you will have one, in today's dollars. Obtain an estimate from your employer.

(Continued)

Downloadable Exhibit 16.1   *(Continued)*

Step 5: $_____
Annual amount needed to close the gap (Step 2 − Steps 3 and 4).

Step 6: $_____
Current retirement savings, including all retirement-plan accounts, any other corporate savings plans, plus savings/investments in regular accounts. (Do not include life insurance.)

Step 7: Select the 4 percent inflation multiplier from the table below based on the number of years until you retire:

Years Until Retirement	Inflation Multiplier
1	1.04
2	1.08
3	1.12
4	1.17
5	1.22
8	1.37
10	1.48
13	1.67
15	1.80
18	2.03
20	2.19

Step 8: $_____
Your annual income goal during retirement (Step 2 × Step 7).

Step 9: $_____
Annual income shortfall at retirement (Step 5 × Step 7).

Step 10: $_____
How much additional capital you'll need during retirement (Step 9 × the suitable multiplier below).

Years in Retirement	Your Assumed Investment Return During Retirement		
	6%	7%	8%
15 years	13.17	12.39	11.67
20 years	16.79	15.47	14.31
25 years	20.08	18.15	16.49
30 years	23.07	20.47	18.30

Step 11: $_____

How much your defined benefit pension (if you have one) will be worth at retirement (Step 4 × the inflation multiplier at Step 7).

Step 12: $_____

How much your current nest egg will be worth at retirement (Step 6 × the applicable multiplier from the table below).

Years Until Retirement	Your Assumed Investment Return				
	6%	7%	8%	9%	10%
1	1.06	1.07	1.08	1.09	1.10
2	1.12	1.14	1.17	1.19	1.21
3	1.19	1.23	1.26	1.30	1.33
4	1.26	1.31	1.36	1.41	1.46
5	1.34	1.40	1.47	1.54	1.61
6	1.42	1.50	1.59	1.68	1.77
8	1.59	1.72	1.85	1.99	2.14
10	1.79	1.97	2.16	2.37	2.59
12	2.01	2.25	2.52	2.81	3.14
14	2.26	2.58	2.94	3.34	3.80
16	2.54	2.95	3.43	3.97	4.59
18	2.85	3.38	4.00	4.72	5.56
20	3.21	3.87	4.66	5.60	6.73

Step 13: $_____

How much you need to save and invest by retirement (Step 10 + Step 11 − Step 12).

Step 14: $_____

How much you need to save and invest annually (Step 13 × the multiplier from the table below).

Years to Retirement	Your Assumed Investment Return				
	6%	7%	8%	9%	10%
1	.9434	.9346	.9259	.9174	.9191
2	.4492	.4429	.4368	.4307	.4248
3	.2852	.2799	.2747	.2696	.2646
4	.2037	.1989	.1943	.1898	.1854
5	.1552	.1508	.1466	.1425	.1385
6	.1232	.1191	.1152	.1114	.1077
8	.0838	.0802	.0768	.0735	.0704
10	.0607	.0576	.0546	.0517	.0490
12	.0459	.0431	.0404	.0379	.0355

(*Continued*)

Downloadable Exhibit 16.1   (*Continued*)

Years to Retirement	Your Assumed Investment Return				
	6%	7%	8%	9%	10%
14	.0357	.0331	.0307	.0285	.0264
16	.0283	.0260	.0238	.0219	.0200
18	.0228	.0207	.0188	.0170	.0154
20	.0186	.0167	.0150	.0134	.0120

Step 15: $_____

Percent of annual income you should save each year (Step 14 ÷ by Step 1).

Note: A blank version of this exhibit can be downloaded from www.trumpuniversity.com/wealth building101 for your personal use.

Source: Copyright: Retirement Wealth Management Inc. Used with permission.

How to Find a Good Stock

Let's start with stocks. As I said earlier, I recommend most people put most of their stock investments in mutual funds and avoid buying individual stocks. However, if you decide to invest the time and effort in doing your own research, there are numerous proven strategies for finding good stocks. These are five of the best:

1. Look for undervalued companies, based on such criteria as low price/earnings ratios or asset value.
2. Seek growth companies that are generating rapid, accelerating earnings per share.
3. Unearth possible "takeover" candidates—companies that may be bought out at a higher price—is a long-term strategy.
4. Invest in "fallen angel" companies that are in the midst of a turnaround.
5. Identify big trends, and the companies that will benefit can also be very profitable.

When I say these and others are "proven" investment strategies, I mean that they have worked over long periods of time. But no single strategy works all the time because different types of stocks become fashionable or go out of favor on Wall Street, sometimes for long periods of time. Even the professional investors who focus on one specific approach or another, such as buying assets cheap or focusing on fast-growth companies, typically go though cycles when their specialties are out of sync with the market. In the late 1990s, for example, large-company growth stocks were the best place to be. In recent years, undervalued smaller companies have led the way.

Regardless of how you choose stocks, I advise you first to be sure that the companies you choose are financially strong, and that they are likely to generate sustained growth of both revenues and earnings over time, despite occasional hiccups and regardless of changing economic conditions.

Good companies come in all sizes and types. By financially strong, I primarily mean companies that have modest long-term debt, giving them maximum flexibility. Many smaller and medium-size growth companies are completely or relatively debt free, but a surprising number of larger blue chips are also virtually debt free. My two favorite examples are Exxon Mobil and Cisco Systems. However, many other fundamentally strong companies may carry significant amounts of debt, yet they generate plenty of cash flow to comfortably handle it.

I'm not suggesting that you never take a blind leap into a hot stock. Most of us like to gamble at least a little, but remember that it is gambling. When you're investing to build your retirement nest egg, you're investing money that you cannot afford to lose. So your focus should be only successful companies that are already making money for their shareholders—no rookies, no story stocks, no gimmicks.

No matter which stock selection approach appeals to you, recognize that it takes quite a bit of time to learn about markets, industries, and companies. As Thomas Jefferson said, and I agree, "I'm a great believer in luck, and I find the harder I work the more I have of it."

How to Pick a Good Mutual Fund

Now let's look at funds. For most of us, traditional mutual funds are the best way to go for at least some of our money. As I mentioned earlier, mutual funds enable you to profit from companies in which you don't have in depth information or experience. There are roughly 8,100 mutual funds out there, with some $10.5 trillion in assets. It's pretty easy to eliminate 85 percent or so of them from serious consideration, but the good ones are well worth looking for and keeping.

Here are the guidelines I follow when selecting mutual funds:

- I look for solid investment results over five years or more.
- Important: The managers who compiled that record should still be at the fund.
- The fund's performance is in at least the upper half, and preferably the top quarter, for all funds of its type.

- I prefer to use funds that take below-average risk compared with the others in its particular fund category.
- Are the funds cheap to buy and hold?

There are some 60 categories of funds ranging from large-company value to small-company growth to emerging markets to high-yield bonds, according to Morningstar, the investment analysis company. Since some types of investments are always doing better than others as conditions evolve, you need to realize that a fund's category will probably have more impact than any other factor on its performance during shorter time periods. An average fund that employs an investment style that's currently strong—undervalued non-U.S. stocks, say—will usually outperform an excellent fund whose holdings are currently out of favor. Until conditions change, that is, which they always do.

Pay Attention to Fees

Low expenses stack the profit odds in your favor. Over many years, low-cost and high-cost mutual funds have performed roughly the same as a group. It's up to you to control your costs. (By the same token, low fees are no guarantee of good performance.)

When you pay a commission or extra management fee, you needlessly lose a chunk of your investment. Never forget that funds sold by brokers, insurance agents, most financial planners and other salespeople always carry some sort of extra cost, in order to compensate the person selling you the fund. This might be an upfront charge, or *load*; a redemption charge, which is deducted from your proceeds when you sell the fund; and/or a hefty management annual fee, some of which is used to pay the financial advisor.

A good rule of thumb is to stick with no-load (sales charge) funds if you're comfortable making your own investment decisions, or if you rely on a fee-only financial planner or investment advisor. Avoid redemption fees. Look for annual expenses of under 1.5 percent for stock funds. For bond funds, low expenses are even more important because bonds tend to return much less than stocks over time. Stick with no-load bond funds that carry annual expenses of well under 1 percent.

BENEFITS OF EXCHANGE-TRADED FUNDS

Now let's look at exchange-traded funds (ETFs), the most popular investment vehicle that Wall Street has introduced in recent years. There are about

430 ETFs in the United States, holding about $430 billion in assets and growing quickly.

ETFs are groups of stocks that track market indexes and stock sectors in the United States and overseas. ETFs now exist for just about every stock market, industry, and investment style. Among the most popular ETFs are those tied to the Standard & Poor's 500, the Dow Jones industrial average, the NASDAQ 100 index, an index of non-U.S. stocks, and a group of equities selected from many emerging markets, such as Hong Kong, Brazil, China, and India.

ETFs offer three main advantages over traditional mutual funds:

1. They provide better trading flexibility. ETF shares trade like regular stocks, at changing prices during the day. Mutual funds are priced only after the market closes.
2. ETFs usually are more tax-efficient than actively managed mutual funds (but not necessarily mutuals that are linked to market indexes). Stock sales by actively managed equity funds can trigger big capital-gains distributions that are taxable in regular accounts (but not tax-deferred retirement plans).
3. Most ETFs carry lower annual management expenses than mutual funds do.

In addition to enabling you to target many stock indexes around the world, ETFs also now increasingly enable you to invest in relatively narrow ways. Among these are commodities and individual currencies. You can also "sell short" (betting on a price decline, market indexes, or industry sectors). But unless and until you know what you are getting into, I advise you to use ETFs for mainstream investment choices rather than very narrow ones by sticking with the most actively traded ETFs.

Now we're ready to look at bonds.

BONDS OFFER A STEADY CHOICE

For bonds, the question of whether to invest in individual issues or funds is somewhat different than it is with stocks. The answer depends primarily on the types of bonds you buy and how much you invest.

When you buy bonds directly, you lock in a yield that brings a steady stream of interest payments, regardless of what happens to interest rates and bond prices. And when you hold a bond to maturity, you'll get the face value back. If you sell your bonds before maturity, the amount you receive depends on interest rates at that time. Bond prices rise when interest rates fall, but bonds decline in value if rates rise.

With bond funds, you cannot lock in a yield. Bond funds have no set maturity because their portfolios change with market conditions, and with the flow of money in or out of the fund. Bond funds are more expensive to hold over time. The average bond fund charges roughly 1 percent of your investment each year. This expense is modest on a smaller investment of, say, up to $20,000, but the more you invest, the more critical extra costs become. On a $100,000 investment, you might sacrifice up to $1,000 of annual interest income by using a bond fund. In addition, bond funds sold by brokers carry either up-front or deferred sales charges, or higher annual expenses. On the upside, though, bond funds own many issues, and you get professional management. Managers can extend and shorten maturities based on their view of what interest rates will do, for example, or seek bonds they consider undervalued.

Investing directly in bonds offers lower expenses and higher yields, but there are drawbacks. Except for Treasury securities, small lots of bonds—$10,000 or less—are expensive to buy and sell. Purchase costs tend to run 1 percent or more of the price, and commissions on sales are even higher. You also limit diversification.

U.S. Treasury securities are the best to buy directly. They carry the highest ratings for credit safety, so you don't have to analyze the issuer's financial health and/or business prospects. So you don't need professional management and diversification.

Treasury bills cost a minimum of $10,000. Two-year and three-year Treasury notes carry a $5,000 minimum. Other issues carry a $1,000 minimum. Treasuries are easy to buy and sell, with low markups and low sales commissions. You can also buy new Treasuries directly at no commission. Visit www.treasurydirect.gov for more information.

Municipal bonds or *munis* are a popular choice for many investors. They, however, often are difficult to buy and sell without high commissions, and can require complex analysis. Buy them directly instead of through bond funds only in these situations:

- You invest at least $50,000, making adequate diversification possible without paying stiff commissions on small purchases.
- You buy high-quality bonds (rated A or higher for financial strength) of well-known issuers.

- You do not plan to make modest additional investments.
- You plan to hold your bonds to maturity.

Municipal bonds or bond funds can be attractive income investments because interest is exempt from federal tax, and usually from state and local taxes, if the buyer lives in the state issuing the bonds. These bonds are particularly appealing to investors in high tax brackets who live in high-tax states.

Municipal bonds pay lower yields, but if you pay federal, state, and/or local taxes on the interest from taxable bonds, you may find that municipals actually generate more net interest income for you than taxable bonds with a higher stated yield. Why? The tax bite on taxable bonds is often greater than the advantage of apparent yields compared with tax-free bonds. Your tax bracket dictates whether tax-exempt investments will give you a higher after-tax yield than fully taxable investments will.

Compare taxable versus tax-free yields with the following formula:

$$\text{Taxable-equivalent yield} = \frac{\text{Tax-free yield}}{1 - \text{Your federal and state tax bracket}}$$

The tax-equivalent yield will be higher for investors in the higher tax brackets. Suppose the yield on a tax-free bond or fund is 4 percent, while the yield on a taxable vehicle is 5 percent, and your federal tax bracket is 28 percent. So 4 percent divided by 0.72 (1 minus 0.28) equals 5.55 percent, which means the municipal investment gives you the higher net yield. If you also pay state income tax at 5 percent, the calculation is 4 percent divided by 0.67 (1 minus 0.33; 28 percent plus 5 percent), which equals a 5.97 percent taxable-equivalent yield.

Here's a quick guide to help you determine if a municipal bond or fund is suitable for you:

Federal tax bracket	Whether appropriate
15 percent	Unlikely
25 percent	Maybe
28 percent	Probably
33 percent	Very likely
35 percent	Very likely

For other types of bonds, such as mortgage and corporate securities, mutual funds generally are your best bet because these types of bond funds often have different characteristics and require extensive analysis.

If you buy bond funds, you can and should minimize expenses by investing in low-cost funds. Vanguard Group charges the lowest amount in the industry and offers a wide variety of well-regarded bond funds, followed closely by Fidelity and T. Rowe Price. Charles Schwab and other discount brokers offer funds from additional fund families at no extra cost.

No matter how you invest, be sure to keep your investment expenses down. This can make quite a difference in your investment return. While you cannot guarantee how your investments will fare, you can control how much you pay for them.

Suppose you have a $250,000 portfolio. If you net 7 percent a year on your investments, $250,000 will grow to $491,787 in 10 years. But if you can keep 1 percentage point more by watching your costs, you will keep an extra $2,500 the first year. If you reinvest each year's savings and earn an 8 percent net return on your investments, you'll end up with $539,731— 9.7 percent more. Think how the differences will add up over 20 to 30 years or more as your investment assets grow.

Like most worthwhile goals, investing for your financial security in retirement won't always be easy. But when you educate yourself and prepare for success by practicing what I've shown you in this chapter, I guarantee that you'll be very pleasantly surprised at the wealth and peace of mind you'll achieve.

For More Information

For investing, read *The Wall Street Journal* (www.wsj.com), and *Investor's Business Daily* (www.investors.com).

To research stocks and mutual funds, visit www.morningstar.com.

To learn about, and buy, U.S. Treasury securities directly, visit www. savingsbonds.gov and www.publicdebt.gov.

To learn about exchange-traded funds, visit the American Stock Exchange (www.amex.com) and Barclay's iShares (www.ishares.com).

17

DIVERSIFY YOUR

INVESTMENT PORTFOLIO

by

Philip A. Springer

In early September 2001, an investor in New Jersey, who I hoped to sign as a client of my wealth-management firm, called me to say that managing his $3 million-plus portfolio was getting too difficult and frankly unpleasant for him. On Thursday, September 6, we met and he signed a contract with us. I told him that the markets were very weak and that he should increase his cash reserves immediately. Fortunately, all of Bob's accounts were already at Charles Schwab, where we manage most of our assets. So we were able to start managing Bob's accounts on Friday, when I sold about $800,000 of his stocks and equity mutual funds.

We all know what happened on September 11, the following Tuesday.

Did I have inside information or a crystal ball? Of course not. I was simply "listening" to what the financial markets were saying. After struggling through the summer, the stock market weakened dramatically in late August, and the selling accelerated in early September. Regardless of the reasons for the sell-off, I knew it was serious and that it was essential to slash my new client's risk immediately, just as I already had done with my other clients. The markets were already weak, making them even more vulnerable to the results of the 9/11 attack.

Over the next six months, I increased Bob's fixed-income investments, sold more equities, and kept his cash reserves high. In March 2002, because of our concerns about the worsening geopolitical situation, we further reduced Bob's equity exposure to under 20 percent, enabling him to largely avoid the dramatic decline of the next six months. We laid low until the spring of 2003, when a new bull market finally began, and then we steadily increased his equity exposure while trimming his cash.

The reason I told you this story is to illustrate that sometimes, there are periods when it's only good sense to set aside an allocation plan and reduce your risk by moving more of your investment wealth to bonds and/or cash. It has nothing to do with trying to outsmart the market, which is impossible. Rather, it's all about lowering your risk, when necessary, to protect yourself.

The world's financial markets offer huge and exciting profit potential. Yet limiting your financial risk is vital in any situation, including investing. Fortunately, disasters almost never happen overnight in the financial markets. They build gradually. For example, the Dow Jones industrial average tumbled a stunning 22 percent on October 19, 1987. But the Dow had already lost 15 percent in the previous nine trading sessions. There was plenty of time for a vigilant investor to protect against catastrophic losses. True, sharp but short declines can occur almost without warning, particularly during a bull market. That's the nature of financial markets. But it's the risk of major loss that you need to be vigilant about.

ALLOCATE FIRST, THEN DIVERSIFY

That's why I want to discuss asset allocation and portfolio diversification in this chapter. If you can grow your wealth at a reasonable rate over time while limiting major losses, the power of compound appreciation will deliver very impressive results for you. To achieve that, you need only do a reasonably good job of allocating your investments assets and diversifying your portfolio.

Many investors spend too much of their time on trying to find the best stock or fund, and not enough time on allocation and diversification. Yet history has shown that asset allocation is the single most important factor in determining your returns from investing. Asset allocation is directly related to risk and potential reward. The second critical element is how you diversify your investments, primarily in equities.

The asset allocation that works best for you depends primarily on your answers to these two questions:

1. *What do I want from my investments?* Asset allocation involves dividing an investment portfolio among different asset categories, typically stocks, bonds and cash. Determine when you'll need to use some or most of your money for living expenses. This might be to make a down payment on a home, invest in a full-time or part-time business, pay college tuition for a child or pay living expenses when you're retired.

2. *How much risk do I want to take?* Risk tolerance is directly related to your investment time horizon, but also to your willingness to take risks in exchange for greater potential returns. Some people are willing to go for broke, while others hate the thought of ever losing money.

The longer your time horizon, the more comfortable you can reasonably feel about investing in more growth-oriented vehicles. Let me explain. When time is on your side, your risk in effect is reduced because the inevitable fluctuations in the market and in the fortunes of individual companies tend to even out over time. And the natural tendency of stock markets is to rise over the long haul, fueled by growing economies and companies. But in the short run, you won't have the time to recover financially if something bad happens. So if you have a shorter-term financial need, minimize your investment risk with that money. What about the investment assets you won't need for 7 to 10 years or more? You can invest for long-term growth and rest easy regardless of short-term fluctuations in the value of your nest egg. So make sure you evaluate your long-term needs and adjust your portfolio accordingly.

Over time, a middle-of-the-road allocation is much better than going to one extreme or the other without the willingness to make adjustments when necessary. For example, many people loaded up on technology stocks in the late 1990s. When the market began its sharp decline in 2000—the worst bear market since the Great Depression—many of these investors refused to sell and suffered dramatic, sometimes life-changing losses.

I also remember hearing of investors who bought 30-year U.S. Treasury bonds after World War II, only to see their principal and the purchasing power of their investment become decimated by rising inflation and interest rates over the next three decades. Yet many held on to those "safe" bonds.

Then there were those savers who enjoyed sky-high yields—12 percent or more—on bank certificates of deposit and money market funds in the early 1980s. "Who needs stocks?", quite a few told me back then. By 1993, though, yields on "risk-free" savings had crashed to 3 percent, which worked out to considerably less than zero after inflation plus taxes on the interest. Meanwhile, the Dow Jones industrial average soared from 850 to 3600.

No single asset allocation is right for everybody. So if you hear somebody from a major brokerage firm on television say, "We currently recommend an allocation of 60 percent stocks, 30 percent bonds, and 10 percent cash," just ignore it.

What, then, is a reasonable asset allocation for you?

- You're single, in your 20s, and investing for retirement 35 to 40 years from now. I think 85 percent or so in stocks generally is okay, with the rest in cash.
- You're 40, married, and with two kids. You're investing for their college educations, your retirement, and your spouse's retirement. An allocation of 70 percent stocks, 20 percent bonds, and 10 percent cash may well be appropriate under typical conditions.
- You're a married couple 10 years from retirement. You might go with something like 60 percent stocks, 25 percent bonds, and 15 percent cash.
- You're about to retire and will need to draw 5 percent or so of your nest egg each year for living expenses. You might have 40 percent in stocks, 40 percent in bonds, and 20 percent in cash.

Periodically, you may also want to "rebalance" your portfolio to bring it back to its targeted allocation mix. Over time, some investments inevitably will grow faster than others, pushing the allocation out of alignment with your investment goals and risk level.

Suppose you want stocks to represent 60 percent of your portfolio, but after a recent stock market increase, they leapt to 75 percent. You can adjust in either of two ways: sell equity investments and use the proceeds to increase the percentages in bonds and/or cash; or make any new investments in bonds while holding other money in cash.

Now let's forget about theory for a minute. How about reality?

From the market peak in 2000 until 2003, when a strong recovery began, the Standard & Poor's 500 index tumbled 46 percent. As an investment advisor responsible for the financial security of my clients, it was my duty to do what I could to protect them. During the dark days of 2001–2002, my clients had as much as 60 percent safely in cash. We survived.

The opposite is equally true. When valuations and risk are relatively low, and the equities market is rising slowly but steadily, as was the case from 2003 through 2006, shouldn't you increase your allocation to equities? At one point in 2006, we were 80 percent-plus in stocks. It was a very good year.

My point is this: You can do well in the financial markets over time by taking a balanced, detached approach. But if you want to make big money, you've got to reach for rewarding opportunities when risk is low—and actively protect yourself when risk is high.

The Securities and Exchange Commission (SEC) offers the conventional wisdom concerning asset allocation. The SEC says that, "Savvy investors typically do not change their asset allocation based on the relative performance of asset categories—for example, increasing the proportion of stocks in one's portfolio when the stock market is hot. Instead, that's when they 'rebalance' their portfolios."

That's a good plan—most of the time. But not always, and those exceptions can make a big difference. History shows that bull markets typically go higher than people expect, and the damage from bear markets can be worse than you might think. If you prefer not too pay much attention to your investments, you may not want to take advantage of good market conditions or protect yourself during downturns. But if you're actively involved, common sense tells you that you should improve your potential rewards when conditions are favorable or limit your risk when the going gets rough.

Here's why: If you don't act early to contain damage to your financial security, the emotional impact from an extended market decline could cause you to react too late—and near the time that a great buying opportunity occurs.

LOOK FOR DIFFERENT TYPES OF STOCKS AND BONDS

Now let's take the management of your investment portfolio a step further and talk about diversification. In addition to allocating your investments among stocks, bonds, cash, and possibly other asset categories, you'll also need to spread out your investments within each asset category. This enables you to reduce risk and perhaps improve your investment returns. The key here is to understand that the various types of stocks and, to a lesser extent, bonds, will perform differently as economic and investment conditions change. As I explained in Chapter 16, "Grow Your Retirement Nest Egg with Stocks and Bonds," different types of stocks and investment approaches go in and out of favor.

In the U.S. stock market, there are more than 5,000 actively traded individual stocks. Many investment analysts divide the U.S. equity market into nine investment-style "boxes." This system consists of three categories of company stock, each with three sizes based on market capitalization (the total value of a company's outstanding common stock).

The three stock categories are:

1. *Value stocks*, generally defined as those with the lowest multiples of price to earnings and book value.
2. *Growth stocks*, which tend to be of the fastest-growing companies, but also the most expensive.
3. *Blend stocks*, which fall between the first two categories; these companies grow faster than value companies, but are less expensive than growth companies.

Morningstar, a leading provider of independent investment research, also measures the risk of these nine categories. It ranks large-cap value, large-cap blend, and mid-cap value as the three most conservative. This is the traditional turf of stocks and mutual funds that are meant to provide varying degrees of growth and dividend income. The mid-level risk grouping is large-cap growth, mid-cap blend, and small-cap value. The highest-risk group consists of mid-cap growth, small-cap growth, and small-cap blend.

Morningstar developed a nine-box grid for bonds, too. The two key characteristics are sensitivity to interest-rate swings and the bond issuers' creditworthiness, which refers to the probability that the issuer will pay the interest and return the principal to investors. Note, though, that default rates are very low for most types of bonds.

The longer a bond's maturity, the more the bond price will change with interest-rate swings. The categories are short, intermediate, and long-term maturity. High-quality bonds are those with credit-quality ratings at or above AA. These are government bonds and the best corporate bonds. Medium quality is from just under A to BBB. Below BBB (or nonrated) is low quality, with higher yields.

Morningstar's analysis of the relative risk of these nine bond categories puts short-term high quality in the lowest rank. Moderate risk consists of intermediate-term high quality, intermediate-term medium quality and short-term medium quality. The riskier bonds are long-term low quality, long-term medium quality, long-term high quality, intermediate-term low quality and short-term low quality.

Careful diversification within the stock and bond allocations enables you to avoid the possibility of large permanent losses while continuing to make good money over time. In addition, if you limit each position to a modest percentage of your nest egg, such as 5 percent for a stock and 15 percent for solid mutual fund, you can relax and take the long-term view your investments deserve.

Relax, yes, but pay attention. It's true that back in the good old days—the great bull market in stocks that that ran from 1982 through early 2000—it generally paid off for investors to buy and hold for the long haul.

But it's different now. Investors need to be more vigilant and proactive than before because the pace of change has accelerated significantly, thanks largely to technological advances in the availability and transmission of information around the world. The rapid flow of information, rumors and opinion can also increase the possibility of investor confusion and uncertainty of today's financial markets.

Frightening? Sometimes, yes. But confusion, uncertainty and even crisis always create fabulous opportunities for profit when you're patient and prepared.

THINK GLOBALLY

Perhaps the biggest change for U.S. investors over the past few years is the coming of age and accessibility of financial markets outside our country. In fact, most of the stock markets in the rest of the world outperformed the U.S. markets by a significant margin in 2004–2006.

This means that when you think about how to diversify your investment assets, stocks, bonds and cash alone aren't enough. In addition to investing in U.S. stocks of various sizes, either directly or through funds, you should include non-U.S. equities too. If you're serious about making money as an investor, you need to view the world as one market, not many.

This shift in orientation is necessary for many reasons. Only 5 percent of the world's population is in the United States, while more than half the world's capital resides outside the United States. The opportunities for economic and investment growth overseas have increased dramatically, in Asia, Europe, and Latin America. In the 1980s, as I recall, roughly two-thirds of the market value of the world's publicly traded companies was in the United States. Now roughly 60 percent is overseas—and close to 75 percent of the world's economic output occurs outside the United States.

You're likely somewhat familiar with China's economic boom, which includes much of the rest of Asia. Japan finally has emerged from a severe economic and investment downturn that lasted 13 years. Latin America offers some of the world's most exciting investment growth possibilities. Even Europe's long-sluggish economies are now improving. Europe's economy is finally creating jobs, underpinning the region's recovery, and helping to strengthen the global economy.

Another reason to look abroad is that we're seeing two huge migrations of capital. In other words, money is moving from the developed world (the United States and western Europe) to the developing world (Asia, eastern

Europe, Latin America). Plus, most foreign stock markets are more attractively priced than the U.S. market, with lower price/earnings ratios (stock price divided by the company's earnings). Often that discount is warranted, for various reasons including superior political stability and accounting standards in the United States. But now we're seeing more good foreign companies than ever before with superior growth and lower valuations than their U.S. counterparts.

What's more, there are now more excellent ways than ever to invest in the rest of the world. For many years, mutual and closed-end funds were the only practical ways to go. In recent years, exchange-traded funds (ETFs) that invest all over the world have become popular.

Also an excellent alternative is American Depositary Receipts (ADRs). An ADR represents a non-U.S. company's publicly traded stock, yet it trades on U.S. exchanges. Investing directly in individual stocks on foreign exchanges has always been cumbersome and expensive (high trading commissions). Today several hundred actively traded ADRs are available to us, and there is plenty of available information about them because foreign companies have to follow many of our rules for accounting standards and financial disclosure in order to meet the listing requirements of U.S. exchanges.

For non-U.S. stocks, the style box system is less structured because of differences in individual markets. But you can still distinguish between large value companies that pay high dividends, say, and smaller, faster-growing companies. Generally, the markets of western Europe are more stable than those of the emerging markets (China, India, Latin America, and so on).

Undeniably, there's a lot to choose from out there. But this doesn't mean you should invest in a bit of everything. Instead, I advise you to spread your investments appropriately among different types of stocks and equity funds, as well as bonds and cash. By appropriately, I mean diversifying only among the types of investments that are suitable for your situation.

For instance, if you won't need any of your investment assets for many years and are a growth investor, you don't need to own bonds for income. If, however, you're a conservative investor, I would never advise you to invest more than token amounts, if that, in small-company growth stocks or emerging markets stocks.

Then, depending on how involved you want to get, you might put higher percentages of your portfolio into types of equities that are doing particularly well, such as large-company growth stocks, mid-cap value stocks, European blue chips and so on.

THINK ABOUT YOUR TIME LINE

Here's another way to approach this important question of what types of stocks and, to a lesser extent, bonds to buy. Consider these guidelines:

- With assets that you won't want for living expenses for 10 years or more, buy stocks or funds that are in the long-term growth categories.
- If you won't have to cash in some of your investments for at least five years, focus on "total return." This means vehicles that pay dividends but are also likely to grow in value over time. I think of this category as "conservative long-term growth."
- For money that you'll need in less than five years, invest it in bonds or bond funds.
- If you'll want to use your money in one year or less, use money market funds.

Okay, let's delve more deeply into diversifying your investment portfolio. Always recognize that you can approach this from different perspectives, and that there are several ways to diversify in order to get where you want to go. Be flexible, not rigid. Remember, investing is more art than science.

At the least, you probably should own individual issues and/or equity funds in three areas: large-company stocks, medium- or small-company stocks, and foreign stocks.

Here are suggestions for three typical situations:

1. *You invest for long-term growth:* U.S. stocks and growth stock funds, 60 percent of your portfolio; international stocks or funds, 30 percent; and cash, 10 percent.
2. *You invest for growth and income:* U.S. equities, 50 percent; international stocks, 20 percent; fixed-income investments, 15 percent; and cash, 15 percent.
3. *You invest primarily for income:* U.S. stocks, 40 percent; international stocks, 15 percent; fixed-income investments, 25 percent; and cash, 20 percent.

As your portfolio grows, the next level of diversification is to buy stocks or funds that employ different approaches: value stocks that are cheap based on assets or current earnings; stocks of companies that are expected to show strong earnings growth; and stocks that generate solid earnings growth and sell at a relatively reasonable price.

A younger person might emphasize earnings growth while a new retiree tilts toward value, yet both could also own investments in the middling growth-at-a-reasonable-price category. The younger person may be more inclined to invest in small-company stocks while the older one goes primarily with large companies. Another way to increase potential returns or reduce risk is to choose relatively aggressive or conservative vehicles, respectively, in a particular category.

Let's talk a little bit about investing for income. This is harder than it used to be. You see, interest rates—and therefore investment yields—fell from the early 1980s until hitting bottom in 2003. Rates have since rebounded to some degree, but they're still relatively low. As I write this, the general rule is that you can get 4.5 percent to 5 percent on your money at little or no risk, and up to about 7 percent with more risk.

Until this general situation changes, in my view, the best solution for the income-oriented investor is to follow a *diversified income program*. This program provides the necessary dividends and interest from a variety of sources, ranging from higher-yielding common stocks to preferred stocks to real estate investment trusts to high-yield bonds to intermediate-term bonds to master limited partnerships.

Also U.S. Treasury notes provide an ideal way to build a "ladder" of different maturities. This increases your flexibility and provides protection against the risk of principal-depressing interest-rate increases. For instance, you might buy notes maturing every year over the next seven, or in every other year—such as 2008, 2010, and 2012. Whichever ladder you choose, you can reinvest the proceeds from maturing T-notes each year or two years in new notes at market rates. This will enable you to boost your income if yields rise.

Investment Styles That Work for You

Now I'll give you specific investments recommendations for each of five different life situations. You're probably in or close to one of them. First, though, a caveat: Very few investments stay good forever. To reduce the risk that my recommendations will already be out of date when you read this, I'm going to focus exclusively on no-load mutual funds run by managers with excellent long-term records. But check out the funds before you invest. Even if you prefer to buy individual stocks or bonds, a great way to learn about investing is to visit fund web sites and research their holdings.

1. *You're 25 years old and single.* After setting aside 10 percent or so for cash reserves, you should invest for long-term growth. So invest your assets as follows:
   Large-company growth and blend: 15 percent
   Mid-cap growth and blend: 20 percent
   Small-cap growth, blend, value: 25 percent
   International: 30 percent
   Cash: 10 percent

2. *You're 35, married, with young children, investing for their college educations and your retirement.* Since each goal has a long time horizon, you should continue to invest for long-term growth. You can keep the same 60-30-10 mix as when you were 25, so you're still in situation 1. Just invest it a little more conservatively, in terms of both category mix and the choices in each category:
   Large-company growth, blend and value: 25 percent
   Mid-cap growth and blend: 20 percent
   Small-cap growth, blend, value: 15 percent
   International: 30 percent
   Cash: 10 percent

3. *You're 45, with two children approaching college age.* Assets earmarked for their educations could be shifted into more conservative funds. For example, shift to bond funds with short average maturities, to provide protection from interest-rate swings.
   But you probably have at least 10 years, and possibly 20, until you retire. So assets you won't need until then should remain in growth-oriented investments. You fall into situation 2:
   Large-company blend and value: 25 percent
   Mid-cap growth, blend and value: 15 percent
   Small-cap blend and value: 10 percent
   International: 20 percent
   Bonds: 15 percent
   Cash: 15 percent

4. *You are in your late 50s, approaching retirement.* You should still be investing for growth and income, but in more conservative categories and individual vehicles:
   Large-company blend and value: 30 percent

Mid-cap blend and value: 20 percent
International: 20 percent
Bonds: 15 percent
Cash: 15 percent ·

5. *You are age 70, and you may well live another 20 years or more.* You may want to reduce your stock-fund exposure. However, even retirees who emphasize high income and capital preservation should hold some stocks in order to generate enough capital appreciation to provide for long-term needs and hedge against inflation. You're in situation 3:

Large-company blend and value: 30 percent
Mid-cap value: 10 percent
International: 15 percent
Bonds: 25 percent
Cash: 20 percent

Here are my three favorite equity mutual funds in each of nine major U.S. categories, plus five international funds, listed from highest risk/reward to most conservative in each group:

- Large-cap growth: Marsico Twenty-First Century, Rainier Core Equity, Harbor Capital Appreciation.
- Large-cap blend: Fidelity Contrafund, Tocqueville, Selected American Shares.
- Large-cap value: Hotchkis & Wiley Large Cap Value, T. Rowe Price Equity Income, Vanguard Wellington.
- Mid-cap growth: Baron Partners, Brandywine, Turner Mid-cap Growth.
- Mid-cap blend: Hodges, Fairholme, Selected Special Shares.
- Mid-cap value: Third Avenue Value, Vanguard Selected Value, Gabelli Asset.
- Small-cap growth: Baron Growth, Janus Venture, Excelsior Small Cap.
- Small blend: RS Partners, Royce Value Plus, Keeley Small Cap Value.
- International: Artisan International, SSGA International Stock, Main stay ICAP International Value, USAA International, Harbor International.

For your Portfolio Management worksheet, visit www.trumpuniversity. com/wealthbuilding101. Investing successfully in the financial markets to build wealth is an incredibly valuable skill. It's also fascinating because it requires a special blend of information—the kind you get through research and knowledge. Keep a healthy balance between the two, throw in a strong dose of commitment, and some patience, and that's it!

VII

PROTECT YOUR WEALTH

18

SAVE MONEY WITH THESE

TAX STRATEGIES

by

J. J. Childers

It doesn't matter where I am—speaking at a seminar, waiting on line at the airport, or even worshipping at church—I hear the same complaint all the time. Eyes light up when I tell folks that I am an asset protection and tax attorney. "I'm paying too much tax," they say, but when I ask, "What are you doing about it?" I get a blank stare.

I've come to expect those blank stares.

Everyone I speak to believes that they pay too much in taxes, and they say that they want to reduce their tax bill, but very few are willing to do what that requires. Some of you may be thinking, Why bother? After all, as Ben Franklin is reputed to have quipped, "There are only two things you can count on—death and taxes."

Why bother? Because taxes are one of the biggest destroyers of wealth in this country. Many reports I've read state that the average American spends more on taxes every year than on food, clothing, and shelter.

Having control over your tax bill can make a great difference in your life and put you on the road to wealth, but you can't take the first step if you're not willing to take action and control the amount of income you now lose every year to unnecessary taxes. You can reduce your tax bill significantly, but you've got to do the work—nobody is going to do that for you.

For most people, realizing that they are, indeed, in control of their taxes is the hard part. It's much easier to blame the problem on someone else. If you don't believe me, think about what I'm saying for a minute, and then ask yourself this question: "What have I done this year to reduce my tax bill?"

It continues to amaze me just how little we know about taxes. Most taxpayers focus almost exclusively on income taxes, and ignore the rest. Most Americans actually look forward to filing their taxes annually because "tax time" means refunds, and refunds mean fun. We take vacations with refunds. We pay down debt. We send the children to school. We splurge on the latest, state-of-the-art audiovisual equipment. I'm asked frequently, "How can I get a larger refund?" Well, the answer is simple, "Pay in more money." The more you pay in; the more you stand to get back. That's the simple mathematical formula accepted by millions of taxpayers. Yet, they're overlooking something very important: A refund is money that you already paid the government. You should be asking this question instead:

How can I pay in less money—and legally keep more of the money I earn?

This chapter is geared toward helping you get enough of a working knowledge about taxes that you can come up with a better strategy than "Pay in more money" to increase your annual refund. Most people don't understand taxes, so let's start with some of the basic facts. Take the following quiz to assess your knowledge of taxes and find out whether you are maximizing your potential deductions. By giving yourself a business check-up, you can keep more of your hard-earned dollars, rather than giving them unnecessarily to your Uncle Sam. (To download your Tax Quiz, visit www.trumpuniversity. com/wealthbuilding101.)

Downloadable Exhibit 18.1   Tax Quiz*

1. When determining your deductible costs for business use of a car, the 2006 standard business mileage rate for passenger automobiles is:
    a. $1 per mile
    b. .25 per mile
    c. .35 per mile
    d. .445 per mile

2. For tax year 2007, self-employed people pay Social Security taxes on the first —————————— they earn.
   a. $42,500
   b. $60,000
   c. $72,500
   d. $97,500

3. The type of tax-advantaged (tax deductible) pension plan for unincorporated small-business owners is referred to as a:
   a. 401(k) plan
   b. Roth IRA
   c. SEP plan
   d. 403(b) plan

4. For self-employed individuals in 2007, what percentage of your health insurance expense is deductible?
   a. 25%
   b. 45%
   c. 50%
   d. 100%

5. The highest federal income tax rate applicable to individual taxpayers is:
   a. 36%
   b. 39.6%
   c. 35%
   d. 50%

6. The profits of which of the following business entities will not be taxed at the owners' individual income tax rates?
   a. Sole proprietorships
   b. Partnerships
   c. Corporations (other than S corporations)
   d. Limited liability companies

7. In an IRS audit, the best kind of evidence to provide in order to prove your business is:
   a. Receipts and canceled checks
   b. Computerized records
   c. Statements from your accountant
   d. Eyewitness testimony

8. All businesses having inventories must use the accrual method of reporting purchases and sales. (True or False)

9. James, a cash-basis salesperson, received commissions in February of 2007 for sales made during the last quarter of 2006. The commissions should be reported on his 2006 tax return. (True or False)

(continued)

Downloadable Exhibit 18.1   (*Continued*)

10.   A cash-basis taxpayer may not claim a bad debt deduction unless the amount to be deducted has previously been included as income. (True or False)

Answers:

1.   d—The standard mileage deduction is .445 per mile
2.   d—$97,500
3.   c—SEP
4.   d—100%
5.   c—35%
6.   c—Corporations other than S corporations
7.   a—Receipts and canceled checks
8.   True—Businesses with inventories cannot use the cash-basis method of accounting
9.   False—Compensation generally must be reported as income in the year received
10.   True—Cash-basis taxpayers typically cannot take such a deduction because money is normally not included in income until it is received

Note: A blank version of this exhibit can be downloaded from www.trumpuniversity.com/wealthbuilding101 for your personal use.

UNDERSTAND WHAT YOU'RE UP AGAINST

Your accountant may tell you that you are in a 15 percent or 25 percent tax bracket, but that's not the whole story. If you've ever received a paycheck, you know that your employer takes taxes out of your pay, but few people know what they are, exactly, and at what rate they are withheld. In this country, we're used to living off the "net" income we receive after taxes; we don't receive 100 percent of what we earn because our employer is required by law to pay taxes on our behalf and withholds money from our paychecks. I've often said that if we wanted true tax reform in the United States, we would do away with tax withholding and make every taxpayer actually write a check to Uncle Sam every pay period. If you did that—if you saw just how much withholding you actually pay—you would be incredibly motivated to reduce your tax bill as quickly as possible.

In looking at the taxes that are deducted from your paycheck, you will see generally four types:

1. Federal income,
2. Social Security,
3. Medicare, and
4. State income.

In some states, additional taxes are withheld, but for purposes of this chapter, we will focus on these four types of withholding.

Federal income tax is withheld based on how you fill out your W-4 income tax form for your employer. As you may know, your marital status, the number of your dependents, and the size and extent of your itemized deductions (mortgage interest, state and local taxes, and charitable contributions) determine your personal tax rate. Current federal individual tax rates range from zero to 35 percent.

Currently, *Social Security tax* is withheld at the rate of 6.2 percent on the first $97,500 of W-2 eligible wages, with employers contributing another 6.2 percent, for a total of 12.4 percent. If you own your own business, however, the IRS considers you both employee and employer, and you contribute the full amount.

Medicare tax is currently withheld from your paycheck at 1.45 percent of your earnings and your employer pays 1.45 percent. Unlike Social Security tax, Medicare tax isn't capped at a certain earnings threshold; every dollar you earn, no matter how little or how much, is subject to Medicare tax. Like the Social Security tax, however, if you are self-employed, you must pay the total of 2.9 percent; 1.45 percent as employer and 1.45 percent as employee.

The combination of Social Security (12.4 percent) and Medicare taxes (2.9 percent) are referred to as the self-employment, or Federal Insurance Contributions Act (FICA) tax, and add up to 15.3 percent.

I stress these numbers because I know that many of you reading this book are looking for new ways to generate income and build wealth and, often, you'll begin this process while maintaining a fulltime job until your new business can begin supporting you. Yet, the extra taxes you pay to become self-employed are a big disincentive in starting a business.

I assume that most readers are in the 25 percent federal income tax bracket, like most working Americans. Let's assume for the moment that you are in that bracket, and you have just started a business. That means your self-employed earnings will be taxed at a federal rate of 25 percent. Including self-employment taxes, you'll pay at least 40.3 percent. If, however, you live in some states, you'll pay over 50 percent because of the additional state income tax. The top five offenders are Montana (11 percent); Rhode Island (10.098 percent); Vermont (9.5 percent); California (9.3 percent); and Oregon (9 percent).

Gaining a working knowledge about taxes doesn't mean you'll avoid paying taxes altogether, but avoid paying as much tax as allowed by law. By understanding the different types of income, and how these types are taxed, you can hold onto more of your hard-earned dollars. Knowledge equals power, and in this case, knowledge equals money.

Not all income is created equally and, more importantly, not all income is taxed equally. To illustrate this point, let's take a look at the following fictitious example.

Tax Planning with Fred and Wilma

Example 1

Facts:

Fred and Wilma are married and combined make $70,000 in wages.

Their itemized deductions and personal exemptions equal $20,000.

They live in a state with a 7 percent income tax rate.

Federal income tax	$6,800.00	
State income tax	$3,500.00	
Social Security and Medicare	$5,355.00	
Tax burden	$15,655.00	22 percent

Example 2

Facts:

Fred is employed by an excavating company and earns $55,000 per year.

Wilma is employed as a fashion designer and earns $60,000 per year.

Their itemized deductions and personal exemptions equal $30,000.

They live in a state with a 7 percent income tax rate.

Federal income tax	$14,870.00	
State income tax	$5,950.00	
Social Security and Medicare	$8,798.00	
Tax burden	$29,618.00	26 percent

Example 3

Facts:

Fred is self-employed by an excavating company and nets $55,000 per year.

Wilma is self-employed as a fashion designer and earns $60,000 per year.

Their itemized deductions and personal exemptions equal $30,000.

They live in a state with a 7 percent income tax rate.

Federal income tax	$12,839.00	
State income tax	$5,950.00	
Social Security and Medicare	$16,249.00	
Tax burden	$35,038.00	30 percent

Example 4

Facts:

Fred leases an office building to an excavating company and has a taxable net of $55,000.

Wilma invests in real estate and earned $60,000 in capital gains.

Their itemized deductions and personal exemptions equal $30,000.

They live in a state with a 7 percent income tax rate.

Federal income tax	$8,875.00	
State income tax	$5,950.00	
Social Security and Medicare	$0.00	
Tax burden	$14,825.00	13 percent

If you study these examples closely, you will see some alarming differences. In Example 2, Fred and Wilma's income increases 64 percent from their income in Example 1, from $70,000 to $115,000, but their tax burden grows much more—almost doubling, from $15,665 to $29,618. In Example 3, they earn the same amount ($115,000) as in Example 2, but pay even more in taxes, $35,038. Yet, in Example 4, the couple earn as much income as they do in Examples 2 and 3, but pay significantly less in taxes.

The reason? Different types of income require different types of tax treatment. Knowing this will give you more choices in deciding how to earn your income and how to build wealth. Now let's take a closer look at these different types of income.

Earned income is income you earn for your personal services and is subject to both income tax and self-employment tax (Social Security and Medicare). The most common type of earned income is W-2 wages. Net income from a self-employed business (filed on Schedule C) is also considered earned income. You want to minimize or avoid earned income as much as possible because it is taxed most heavily.

Passive income is income that you generate from something other than personal services. Passive income is subject to income tax, but not self-employment tax. The most common type of passive income is rental property because the income generates from the value of your property, not the value of your personal services. You can also generate passive income from your personal involvement, or lack thereof, in your business. Certain business entities such as limited partnerships can create passive income. We'll talk more about these a little later.

Portfolio income is income you earn on your investments. This type of income includes interest, dividends, and capital gains. This type of income is subject to income tax, but not self-employment tax and, in this way, is similar to passive income. There's one big difference, though, between passive and portfolio income: you pay less tax on portfolio income when you generate capital gains, which currently are taxed at a maximum rate of 15 percent.

Sooner or later, I believe this preferential rate will expire, so take advantage of it now. High-end taxpayers understand this, and won't let this break pass without taking full advantage of it. You shouldn't either. If there's an investment you've been holding onto, but were afraid to sell because of high capital gains taxes, now might be the time to sell if you can maximize your overall return.

Deferred income is income on which you don't currently pay tax, but will at some point in the future. Retirement plans are an easy way to set up deferred income; you take a current deduction today for the amount you contribute to your retirement plan, but pay tax when you withdraw money at retirement. Hopefully, that will be many years from now, when you may be in an even lower tax bracket than you are currently.

A Section 1031, or similar, exchange is another way to generate tax-deferred income. You can sell a piece of property at a gain, but defer the tax by acquiring another investment property. There are certain parameters you must meet, and tax-savvy investors are smart to study all the ins and outs of Section 1031 exchanges.

Tax-free income is exactly that—tax free. It's smart to know the ways you can achieve tax-free income. Let's say you are beginning to earn more income. That's great, but now you'll have to pay more tax; 35 percent in federal taxes, and 7 percent in state, for a total of 42 percent. You shop long and hard for a good money market rate, and find one that pays 6 percent. Unfortunately, much of that interest income—about 40 percent—is lost in income taxes, and you end up with an effective gain of 3.6 percent, a little more than half of what you had hoped to yield. Tax-free investments may yield lower returns, but at a higher tax rate than many after-tax investments. One example most working Americans are familiar with is the onetime break they get from the federal government when they sell their personal residence. If you use a home as your main, or principal, residence for any two out of the preceding five years, any gain is tax-free, up to the first $250,000 for single filers, or $500,000 for married filers. Adding a few thousand or more tax-free dollars to your portfolio from the sale of your house is a smart move that can generate wealth at an amazing clip.

In giving you this quick overview on the different types of income, my purpose is to help you begin to understand that you can change the amount of taxes you pay by changing the way you earn income. You have no control over the type of tax you pay, or the amount of tax, when you work for an employer, but you can dramatically lower your tax bill by changing the nature of the income you receive. Look at Fred and Wilma. They earned the same amount of income in Examples 2, 3, and 4, but their taxes varied dramatically. I constantly challenge my clients to look for ways to generate types of income that will yield preferential tax treatment for them. I want to help you do the same.

Making Tax Changes Means Making More Money

By now, I hope that you're starting to realize that you must make some changes if you want to improve your tax situation. In the previous section, we discussed how different types of income can benefit you. Now I want to talk about how changing your taxpayer status can benefit you.

A working knowledge of this subject can help you map out a plan to cut your tax bill significantly.

Individuals

We're used to being individual taxpayers; that's our default status. If you do nothing to change this status, however, you will be taxed at your full income tax rate and, in addition, the full 15.3 percent self-employment tax when you start or buy your own business. Obviously, that is not a preferred status. If you're content with your current tax situation, stop reading here; if not, keep reading.

General Partner

If you are a general partner, you have the same tax status as an individual taxpayer, which means that you will pay full income tax in whatever bracket you are in, and, in addition, the full 15.3 percent self-employment tax. Merely going into business with others does not help you save taxes on the income generated from the business.

As an example, let's assume you took your W-2 to your accountant to prepare your taxes. The W-2 reports that you earned $30,000. You work hard, you pay your bills, but no one would consider you rich. When your accountant finishes taking deductions for you and your family, the odds are that you owe no income taxes and receive back all the income tax you paid.

Now assume you have your own business. You bring your accountant all of your income and expense receipts, and when they finish calculating deductions, your net income from the business is $30,000, which means you will owe no income taxes. You can't, however, deduct expenses such as mortgage interest and charitable contributions, and you will have to pay 15.3 percent, or $4,500 in self-employment taxes, on the entire net income of $30,000. Is $4,500 a big deal to someone who earns $30,000 a year? I'd say so. My guess is you're reading this book because you want to make significantly more than $30,000. Hopefully, this spells out the problem. Let's start to find some solutions.

Limited Partner

A limited partner is invested, but not involved, in a business. Their share of income is based on his or her investment, not their personal services, so they don't pay self-employment tax. We could spend hours discussing the different ways to use limited partnerships, but they are very complicated. For our purposes here, it's enough for you to realize that the use of limited partnerships can significantly reduce your self-employment taxes.

S Corporation Shareholders

An S corporation shareholder is another type of taxpayer defined in the Internal Revenue Code, and it is extremely popular for small businesses where the owner actually works in the business. Unlike individual sole proprietorships and general partnerships, you can save significant amounts of self-employment tax by utilizing these entities because an S corporation shareholder is only liable for self-employment taxes on the amount he or she pays themselves in salary. This creates an opportunity to provide significant savings, compared with the "default" status of individuals and general partnerships.

C Corporations

C corporations provide an opportunity to save taxes by utilizing a concept called *income splitting*. The taxes you pay grow as your income increases. C corporation income is taxed at 15 percent on income up to $50,000, which means that if you are in a 35 percent personal tax bracket, the possibility exists for saving significant tax dollars by redirecting some of that income into a C corporation. You can save on taxes by using a C corporation, but consult with a tax professional before you decide this is right for you.

LLC Members

This chapter would not be complete without a brief mention of limited liability corporations (LLC). An LLC is a combination of a partnership and a corporation, but unlike other types of taxpayers, state, not federal, law creates LLCs. This poses significant problems for state and federal entities in determining exactly how LLCs are taxed, but don't get too excited. You still have to pay tax on LLC income. Currently, the IRS views LLCs in the same context as general partners, and that puts taxpayers in situations where little tax savings occurs. What I am telling you may contradict what your tax professional has said, but that is how the IRS views LLCs. This arrangement, however, is effective for passive income (e.g., renting property), but not good at all for a business in which you actually perform services.

IMPLEMENTING MY TAX SECRETS

I hope I've given you a good introduction to realizing that there are many ways you can significantly reduce your overall tax bill. The IRS looks at the different types of taxes, and taxpayers, differently, which is why you need to understand the distinctions before putting a strategy into place.

My final advice: Start today! It's time to move from complaining about to reducing the taxes you pay, and making more of your money work for you.

There are steps you can take, but you must start taking them for them to help you! Start by changing your tax status, and then move to the greatest tax shelter of all—owning and operating your own small business, which will put you well on your way to becoming, and more importantly, staying wealthy.

For More Information

Visit www.irs.gov/business/small/index.html and www.secretmillionaire.com.

19

PROFIT FROM AN
ESTATE PLAN
by
J. J. Childers

After taxes, there are two big obstacles to keeping the wealth you worked so hard to build. In this chapter, we tackle these two hurdles head-on and clear the way for you to create and implement the estate plan that will distribute your hard-earned assets to your heirs in the way you want.

The first obstacle is the government's relentless attack as wealth passes from one generation to the next. In this chapter, you learn the closely guarded secrets of the super rich about dealing with taxes, fees, and other factors that can prevent you from passing your wealth on to your heirs.

The second obstacle is your own resistance to having an estate plan. Most people don't know what estate planning is, and many mistakenly think estate planning is only for the super rich. Drafting a will is often the only step taken by those who recognize the need for estate planning. A will may certainly be part of an estate plan, but there is a lot more to the process.

To understand any subject, ask yourself six basic questions: "Who?" "What?" "When?" "Where?" "Why?" and "How?" Estate planning is no exception. In thinking about an estate plan, ask yourself:

1. Who needs an estate plan? Who are your heirs?
2. What assets will you leave?
3. Where can you go to get help with your estate plan?
4. When should your assets be passed?
5. Why do you need a formal estate plan?
6. How can you accomplish your estate planning goals?

Then think about this: Some of the highest taxes many Americans pay are those imposed on our estates when we die. If you don't set up a proper estate plan, your heirs, whether your family or a favorite charity may actually be forced to pay taxes on your estate after you die, which defeats or, at the very least, minimizes the assets you worked so hard to accumulate during your lifetime. If you set up a proper estate plan, you can minimize the impact of excessive taxes and change the future for your heirs. You create a lasting legacy, which is a wonderful gift. Take the time now to answer each one of these questions, and then commit yourself to implementing a successful estate plan. To download your Estate Planning Quiz (Exhibit 19.1), visit www.trumpuniversity.com/wealthbuilding101.

Downloadable Exhibit 19.1   Estate Planning Quiz*

1.	Do you have a substantial life insurance policy or policies?	Yes	No
2.	Do you own real property or other tangible assets in multiple states?	Yes	No
3.	Would you like to have a say in who receives the benefit of your hard-earned assets instead of allowing the government to decide?	Yes	No
4.	Have you been told, or do you believe, that you are under this year's estate tax exemption so you don't need to worry about an estate plan?	Yes	No
5.	Do you have minor children you want cared for, according to your directives in the event of your death?	Yes	No

6.	Do you have certain requests regarding your death and interment that you don't want your family to have to deal with in their time of sorrow?	Yes	No
7.	Do you want to have a say in your medical care and treatment, in the event that you are unable to voice your directives to your medical team?	Yes	No
8.	Do you currently have a living trust, will, or other estate plan in place that is more than five years old?	Yes	No
9.	Do you wish to leave parts of your estate to people or organizations not directly related to you or in your line of succession (godchildren, family friends, stepchildren, cousins, charities, alma maters, etc.)?	Yes	No
10.	Do you have elderly family members, children, or stepchildren with special needs for whom you want to provide?	Yes	No
11.	Do you have a blended family with assets and heirs from previous relationships or marriages that you want specifically directed, with as little friction or confusion as possible?	Yes	No
12.	Do you have heirs or beneficiaries who may not be financially responsible, and whom you feel will need an administrator or direction for their inherited assets?	Yes	No
13.	Do you have, or expect to acquire, assets that you would like to continue to control even after your death?	Yes	No

If you answered Yes to three or more of these questions, you should seriously consider beginning the estate planning process. If you answered Yes to five or more of these questions, you must establish your estate plan immediately.

Note: A blank version of this exhibit can be downloaded from www.trumpuniversity.com/wealthbuilding101 for your personal use.

Probably the most frequent question I'm asked is, "Do I really need an estate plan?" One of the most common misconceptions when it comes to estate planning is to not worry if you don't have a lot of assets. Let me state this very clearly: Everyone should have an estate plan because everyone who owns assets has an estate. No matter how big or small your estate is, *everyone* needs to have some sort of estate plan in place to properly distribute their assets, by law, upon their death. If you want to leave your assets to your family, or a favorite charity or cause, you must specify your wishes in a properly established estate plan. Otherwise, a court could determine the distribution of your assets and the care of your dependents in a way that doesn't follow your wishes. The chances are good that the government's wishes may not match your own.

Another misconception about estate planning is that it is only necessary for the purpose of avoiding estate taxes. Many estates, even modest-sized ones, are vulnerable to both state and federal inheritance and/or estate taxes, but that's not why all estates need some degree of estate planning. The main reasons are to:

- Make sure your assets go where you want them to go.
- Control assets while you are alive but incapacitated.
- Control assets after death.
- Minimize the emotional and financial burden on your heirs.
- Minimize feuding among heirs over your estate.
- Increase the amount available for charitable donations.
- Avoid the cost and delay of probate.
- Provide for a guardian of minor children or for elder care.

As you can see, these are all very important considerations that apply to everyone, not only the wealthy.

Another reason that people tend to put off estate planning is that they mistakenly believe that it's not necessary until "later" in life. Nothing could be further from the truth. Different stages of life call for different estate planning strategies.

Like most priorities in our lives, estate planning changes as our life experiences change. When we are young adults, we typically don't think about estate planning. At this stage, we usually have few assets, don't have a spouse or children, and are focused on getting ahead in our careers. As we begin to put down roots, however, estate planning becomes more important to us.

As we grow in experience and assets, our strategies for estate planning change, too. In entering the next stage, our greatest concern is providing for our young families in the event of our death. Since we may not necessarily have many assets we should think about life insurance, which is often rather inexpensive at this point. No one wants to think about death, but that is part of the responsibility of a parent or business owner—to provide for those who depend on us with a comprehensive estate plan.

As your children and, hopefully, your assets grow, your estate plan should grow and become more complex. You may begin adding others to your list of beneficiaries, such as an alma mater, your church, or a charity. As you'll see later in the chapter, there can be tax benefits associated with contributing to charitable causes and organizations as well.

Finally, when you reach your golden years, you may want to add several beneficiaries to your estate plan. You may also want to specify your wishes for your funeral or internment, or your care, should you become incapacitated or unable to care for yourself. Dealing with such end-of-life issues isn't anyone's favorite task, but doing so in the present is the only way to ensure that your wishes are followed in the future.

Once you have put your estate plan strategy into place, your work isn't done yet. Every few years, or annually if your life circumstances or wishes change, you should review your estate plan to be sure it reflects your wishes. As time goes on, your assets can grow and change, and so must your estate plan.

One last word here: Today, you can choose to direct what you want to happen by setting up an estate plan that reflects your wishes. Tomorrow, you may not have the opportunity.

TOOLS FOR ESTATE PLANNING

Now let's look at some of the tools needed to build an effective estate plan. Most of you are probably familiar with a will, which is the most popular form of estate planning. Wills are simply written directives that outline how you want the courts to distribute your assets and provide for your dependents after your death. There's a problem: Wills must still go through the court system in an expensive and time-consuming process called probate, where the court decides if your directives should be followed. A will is essentially just a suggestion to the courts about how you want your assets distributed. In the next section, we'll discuss in more detail why you want to avoid probate. If a will doesn't help you properly plan your estate, what does? A *trust*. A trust is a contract; one person (the Trustor) hands over property to another person (the Trustee), with instructions to hold and manage the property for the benefit of a third party (the Beneficiary). There are many types of trusts to use for estate planning.

Revocable Living Trust

In this type of trust, an individual (Trustor) or a couple (Trustors) transfer legal title of assets from their name(s) to the Trustee(s) of the trust. According to the terms outlined in the Trust document, the Trustee manages the trust property. In most cases, however, the Trustor(s) often act as the initial Trustee(s) of the trust and maintains complete control of the trust during his or her lifetime. In other words, the same person who establishes the trust is also the person who executes, or carries out, the terms of the trust, and can thus continue to buy, sell, borrow, or transfer assets at any time. In addition, the Trustor(s) may change or revoke the disposition of the assets at death, and also change the persons named as Trustees during their joint lifetimes, as long as they are considered competent.

For most of us, the biggest benefit of a Revocable Living Trust is avoiding probate. Without a living trust, your estate (personal assets, business interests, life insurance death proceeds, and government benefits) will have to go through probate. What exactly is probate, and why would I want my estate to avoid it? Probate is the legal process used to finalize an individual's legal and financial affairs after their death. Assets and liabilities of the estate are identified, debts paid, taxes filed, and administrative (i.e., attorney) fees are paid. Any remaining assets are distributed to the beneficiaries of the estate, if provided by a will; if there is no will, they are distributed according to state law.

On the surface, probate sounds like a nice, tidy process, and conceptually it is. However, once attorneys, accountants, and our court system get involved, this process can become a nightmare. Probate creates several problems:

- Your estate can be drained by up to 10 percent of its value in administrative expenses, legal fees, debts, and court costs, leaving your beneficiaries with much less than what you intended them to receive.
- The court—not you—may determine the final distribution of your estate and the guardianship of any dependents, whether you have a will or not.
- Your heirs may not receive any assets for months, or even years, and suffer financial strain if your estate has to be probated.
- Your assets become a matter of public record, which exposes your assets to heirs' creditors, friends, neighbors, and even ex-spouses, who can choose to use the probate process to "contest the will" and demand your assets.
- If your estate has to be probated, that's not the end of it. There are still estate taxes, property taxes, income taxes, accounting fees, and more legal fees to pay in addition to probate costs that will continue to drain your estate.

The solution? Don't choose probate, which is the "default" option that you're stuck with if you don't plan and execute a living trust. Choose a trust.

A trust makes sure your wishes—and assets—pass on to loved ones and beneficiaries as you wish.

Now let's talk about a few ways to legally reduce, or perhaps even eliminate, estate taxes.

A Revocable Living Trust is probably the most frequently used trust in estate planning. In addition to avoiding probate, if you are married and establish a trust together, the trust can receive an estate tax exemption of $4 million, through what's called an "A-B" provision. If you don't have a properly executed trust, you'll only receive $2 million—half of what your estate could have received.

Charitable Remainder Trust

Another popular trust is the *Charitable Remainder Trust* (CRT). This type of trust serves three main purposes:

1. Benefits a charity of your choice.
2. Receives a current year tax deduction.
3. Provides an income stream for you and your spouse for life.

Often wealthy individuals realize that they and their children and grandchildren have enough money to live a lifetime of wealth, and set up a CRT to benefit a charity and save on unnecessary taxes. In this type of trust, you donate to the trust property (real estate, stocks, bonds, investments, cash, or the sale of a business interest) for the benefit of the charity. During your lifetimes, you and your spouse receive an income tax deduction equal to the fair market value of the transferred property, and also income from the CRT. After you both pass, the charity receives the remainder of the trust. This is a great way to help a worthy cause, while helping yourself, too. It's a true win-win situation.

Spendthrift Trust

Another popular trust used for estate planning is the *Spendthrift Trust*. This type of trust is established usually for the benefit of a minor child, fiscally irresponsible adult child, or perhaps an elderly parent, who depends on you for financial support or can't manage his or her own finances.

Assets placed in such a trust never become the property of the beneficiary, who receives only income from the trust. Because a beneficiary never can receive the assets in the trust, neither can creditors, which provides an asset protection benefit for your estate as well.

Irrevocable Life Insurance Trust

If you have a great deal of life insurance, another type of trust to consider is an *Irrevocable Life Insurance Trust* (ILIT). The ILIT is established as the owner of a life insurance policy, so that estate taxes are avoided by putting the payout from the life insurance policy into a trust rather than the decedent's taxable estate.

If you have several small life insurance policies from forgotten sources (your employer, your mortgage, private policies, through clubs or memberships in certain associations), it may be a good idea to put the larger one(s) into an ILIT, because the smaller ones can quickly add up and could push you over the estate tax exclusion. These types of trusts are complex and must be done properly to avoid the estate tax issues. Seek the assistance of a reputable professional or firm. If an ILIT is improperly established or maintained, the life insurance policy payout can be revoked or– worse and most likely– included in the decedent's estate, where it then becomes subject to taxes if the size of the assets put your estate over the estate tax exclusion.

Gifting

Gifting is another frequently used method in estate planning. This involves giving your heirs or beneficiaries annual gifts during your lifetime that thus move assets out of your taxable estate before your death.

There are limits as to what you can give to each heir, each year, without taxes, but if done properly, it can effectively move thousands of dollars out of your taxable estate, and can also give you the joy of helping heirs with gifts of cash or assets for major expenses such as financing college, buying a home, and raising grandchildren. Once again, this gives us a way to help others while helping ourselves. This is another win-win situation.

Remember, you need expert guidance to establish an estate plan. Laws change frequently, and tools can be extremely complex. One misstep could cost you more stress and expense than not having an estate plan at all. Establishing a lifelong relationship with estate planning professionals who can guide and assist you with your plan is a must in your wealth-building "To-Do" list. Properly planned and implemented, an estate plan can be one of the most important gifts you give to your heirs.

LEAVE BEHIND THE BLUEPRINTS

As mentioned at the beginning of this chapter, you must answer six questions before you start the estate planning process. (Why do you need a formal estate plan? Who are your heirs, or beneficiaries? What assets will you leave? Where can you go to get help with your estate plan? When should your assets be passed? How can you accomplish your estate planning goals?) This is very important, which is why I am mentioning this again. Once you define your goals and objectives, you are ready to sit down and draw up a detailed design or blueprint of your financial position.

FIVE ESTATE PLANNING STEPS

There are the five basic, and successive, steps necessary to create and maintain your estate plan:

1. *Document.* You and your financial professional(s) assemble all the pertinent facts about your material resources and assets. In addition, look at the personal and financial habits and circumstances of family members or potential heirs. Take into account both past and potential behavior, family changes (marriage, births, divorce, deaths, etc.), financial status and responsibility as objectively as possible.
2. *Analyze.* Analyze these facts and compare them against your goals and objectives.
3. *Formulate.* Formulate several potential plans, then play devil's advocate and test them. Select the one that will help you reach your estate planning goals.
4. *Implement.* No plan can be successful unless it is implemented.
5. *Review and revise.* Perform periodic reviews. Revise the estate plan every three to five years, on average, or more or less frequently as your life changes.

Now that you have consulted with a professional and established, implemented, and funded your estate plan, make sure it is kept current with your changing life situation and reviewed frequently. Equally as important, make sure others know that you have a plan in place. If you have a medical directive or living will as part of your Revocable Living Trust, but no one brings it to the attention of your doctors, it will not do you any good. Likewise, funeral or internment instructions that are not found until after the service were wasted efforts. Keep a copy of the trust document with your estate planning professional, and put the original in a secure place (i.e., a deposit box, vault or fireproof file cabinet). Give copies of your medical directive to your primary physician for your file, and also provide one to a hospital or medical center before any type of surgery or treatment.

A simple, commonsense way to make sure your wishes are followed is to share your wishes with loved ones. I don't mean telling them the specifics, but letting them know that you have a plan in place, and the name of your estate planner, is a must. Also list and describe all items of value, including those relating to family history, and any liquid assets, such as cash or bearer bonds. It's great to hide "mad money" in a secret compartment of a desk or dresser, but if those assets are sold or destroyed after your passing, that "mad money" will never benefit anyone.

To summarize: Everyone needs an estate plan. Put the plan in place, and then move your assets into that plan. Your plan may be as simple as a Revocable Living Trust, or it may be designed with all the additional benefits and complexities of CRTs, ILITs, gifting, or a spendthrift trust because of your individual goals and needs. By establishing an estate plan, you take advantage of the law to provide for and care for your loved ones after you pass. You create a legacy that will continue for generations to come, through the assets you leave behind.

Think about it. Estate planning is really one of the most empowering steps you can take to secure wealth now and for years to come. That can't happen if you don't take action.

As Ben Franklin said, "Those who fail to plan, plan to fail." Decide to start planning your estate now. It will make a big difference, in your life and the lives of those you love.

For More Information

Visit these federal agency web sites (www.mymoney.gov and www.pueblo. gsa.gov).

Also, check out the American Association of the Retired Persons (www. aarp.org), and the Social Security Administration (www.ssa.gov).

20

PROTECT YOUR ASSETS
by
J. J. Childers

In this final chapter, we're going to talk about a phenomenon that has a big impact on wealth building. In fact, if you're not paying attention, all your hard work can disappear with the snap of a finger.

Or more likely, the flick of a judge's order. I'm talking about a phenomenon that I've heard referred to as the "lawsuit explosion." Reports I've read state that there over 75,000 new lawsuits filed every week in this country.

It's hard to build wealth—but harder to hold onto your financial assets if you don't protect yourself from legal threats by installing an *asset security system* to safeguard both your business and personal assets.

Stop and think for a moment. Are you protected? Have you been so busy building wealth that you haven't protected yourself from frivolous lawsuits? If so, you better have your checkbook handy. Even if you win the lawsuit, defending yourself and your business can cost from a low of $50,000 up into the seven-figure range.

Why do so many individuals and businesses get sued? The answer is simple: money.

Here's an example. Suppose you're involved in a car accident, suffer a broken arm, and miss work for a week. Obviously, you're going to have medical bills, lost income, and maybe incur some pain and suffering. You may feel that you have the right to recover damages from the person who caused the accident, so you walk into an attorney's office. The attorney will decide whether to take your case, not by how much you suffered, but by how much money can be gained by suing the person who caused your accident.

Now let's turn the tables. Suppose you own a trucking company, and one of your trucks gets into a minor fender bender with another motorist. At the scene of the accident, the motorist has no injuries whatsoever, but once he gets home, he might decide to feign an injury, sometimes referred to as an IRL (Individual Retirement Lawsuit). In this scenario, his attorney will decide that a lawsuit is a good idea by looking at the size of your pockets. Unfortunately, this deep-pocket theory is the unofficial legal standard that a lot of attorneys follow, so you've got to be prepared.

In deciding if a plaintiff can get his hands on your assets, here's what an attorney will determine:

- *Can assets can be reached?* (by filing a lien on your property, garnishing, or legally accessing, your future wages, or forcing the sale of assets?)
- *Can assets be located?* Many times, a shrewd individual or business will hold their assets in the name of a friend or spouse, in a corporation (or corporations), in a trust, or even outside the country, making them difficult to locate.
- *Can my plaintiff win?* That's the final consideration—if the answer is yes, you'd better be prepared.

The first, and easiest, step in formulating an asset protection plan is to take advantage of available exemptions. An exemption is a law that states that certain property is exempt from the reach of creditors. The most common type of exemption is the *homestead exemption*. If creditors sue you, or in the event of a bankruptcy, your home is protected up to a certain dollar amount. This amount varies by state. Other types of exemptions include:

- Retirement plan exemptions
- Wage exemptions
- Annuity exemptions
- Tools of the trade exemptions (tools, computers, books, etc.)
- Household goods exemptions
- State-specific exemptions (check with your lawyer for these)

In taking advantage of exemptions, there are two goals:

1. *Identify and retain ownership of assets that qualify for an exemption.* A classic example is claiming the homestead exemption by keeping your home in your personal name.
2. *Convert assets from those that do not qualify for an exemption into assets that do.* A common example is to liquidate nonexempt assets and invest that money in a home. This is more complex, and you must be careful to avoid any actions that can be considered fraudulent. We will discuss fraudulent transfer later in the chapter. *Caution*: The rules on such transfers or conversions of assets vary greatly from state to state, so always consult with an attorney in considering this strategy.

Now let's take a look at some of the specific components. Before deciding which type of business entity is right for you, understand how these different types work:

- Sole Proprietorship
- General Partnership
- C Corporation
- S Corporation
- Limited Liability Company
- Limited Partnership

Let's look at each in turn.

A *sole proprietorship* is the most popular type of business structure, because they are simple and inexpensive to set up and maintain, and do not require a business owner to comply with statutory requirements. The business owner does not have to form the entity with the Secretary of State, or file any annual reports. Unless a business is specifically formed as a distinct legal entity, such as a corporation or a limited liability company, your business is automatically a sole proprietorship by default.

While this type of option may seem desirable at first glance, I never recommend this type of business entity. The business owner is personally responsible for any debts or liabilities of the business, which means that you have no protection from creditors seeking assets. Sole proprietorships are just too risky.

A *general partnership* is a sole proprietorship with more than one owner, with each owner sharing in the management of the partnership. Like a sole proprietorship, any creditors of the general partnership can seek assets from any and all individual owners.

C and *S corporations* are the next choice. A corporation has a legal existence separate and distinct from its owners (shareholders). Generally a corporation is in existence perpetually until the owners decide to dissolve the corporation, or legal action forces the corporation to dissolve. A corporation is a popular choice because of the asset protection it affords; generally speaking, as a legal "person" separate and distinct from its owners, any debts or liabilities belong only to the corporation.

The next type of business entity we'll discuss is the *limited liability company*, or LLC. An LLC is a hybrid between a partnership or sole proprietorship and a corporation. Like owners of a general partnership or a sole proprietorship, LLC owners report business profits or losses on their personal income tax returns, because the LLC is not a separate taxable entity. Like a corporation, however, any debts and obligations that owners incur are their own, separate and distinct from the other owners of the LLC.

The final business entity we'll discuss is the *limited partnership*, or LP. You'll recall from our earlier discussion on general partnerships that each partner has the right to participate in the management of the partnership, and is also personally liable for the debts and liabilities of the partnership. With a limited partnership, however, the partners (except for general partner), do not participate in the partnership's day-to-day activities, and are only "at risk" for their own investment in the partnership. A general partner controls the partnership, but is personally responsible for debts and liabilities, in contrast to a limited partner, who has no managerial control and is only personally liable for the amount of their investment.

Which entity is right for you will depend on several variables, such as your marital status, your age, whether you have children, and whether you own one, or several, businesses. Discuss your decision with your accountant or attorney, so they can properly advise you on the legal and tax consequences for each entity. To download your Asset Protection Quiz (Exhibit 20.1), visit www.trumpuniversity.com/wealthbuilding101.

Downloadable Exhibit 20.1   Asset Protection Quiz to Determine Vulnerabilities in Your Personal Financial Plan*

Do you operate a business as a partnership or sole proprietorship?	_____ Yes	_____ No
Do you own any rental properties in your name?	_____ Yes	_____ No
Do you expect your wealth to grow measurably in the next five years?	_____ Yes	_____ No

Are any of your assets listed in the public record under your personal name? _____ Yes _____ No

Is the equity in your home greater than the homestead exemption in your state? _____ Yes _____ No

Would you like to structure your wealth in a way to reduce your income and estate taxes? _____ Yes _____ No

Do you own a liability insurance policy that protects the total value of your wealth? _____ Yes _____ No

Do you have a business that owns its own equipment? _____ Yes _____ No

Have you saved significant assets for your retirement? _____ Yes _____ No

Are you engaged in a high-risk profession such as medicine or real estate? _____ Yes _____ No

Assets that belong in a Living Trust

- Personal residences
- Retirement accounts such as IRAs or 401(k)s
- Vehicles used for personal transportation or recreation, such as cars, trucks, motorcycles, or boats
- Personal property, such as jewelry, furniture, or electronics
- Investment accounts and/or assets held for personal investments, such as stocks and bonds

Assets that should be owned by a corporation, LLC, or LP

- Any real estate that is not used as a primary residence
- Any businesses you own, either as a sole proprietorship or partnership
- Rental properties
- Tools of the trade (i.e., restaurant equipment, vehicles, office machinery, or other assets used primarily to conduct business)
- Business inventories (including real estate, if you expect to buy and sell more than three properties in one year)

*Note: A blank version of this exhibit can be downloaded from www.trumpuniversity.com/wealth building101 for your personal use.

LAYERING AN ASSET PROTECTION PLAN

Now that you understand some of the asset protection benefits of individual business entities, you might be anxious to put all of your assets into one entity—but hold on. In my experience, using multiple entities is the smart way to go. To put a sound asset protection strategy into place, it's smart to "layer" your entities to afford your assets maximum security.

What does layering mean? Whenever I explain this concept, I like to use an analogy you've probably heard. It's not smart to put all your eggs in one basket because, if you lose that one basket, you lose all your eggs. The process of layering your business entities to maximize asset protection is roughly the same. If you set up a legal business entity and are sued, the judgment holder won't be able to touch your personal assets. They will, however, be able to reach the entity's assets, so if you put all your "eggs" into that one entity, you will have a huge hole in your asset protection fortress.

How many entities should you use? That depends on these considerations:

- How much of your total net worth is the asset or assets do you want to protect?
- How much equity do you have invested in the asset? As an example, say you have three rental properties, and all three are fully mortgaged. In this case, there would be little harm in placing all three in the same entity because, if the entity is sued, you haven't lost that much (except for rental income). If, however, one property has a lot of equity, then it's smart to put that property into a separate entity.
- How do you use your assets? Are one, or more, high risk? Say you have three businesses: an ice cream stand, a flower shop, and a dynamite factory. Which business do you think has the greatest chance of being sued? Of course, the dynamite factory. That asset should be held in a separate entity.

To summarize at this point: You can create multiple entities to hold your assets. In addition, there are these strategies:

- *Use more than one entity to own a single business.* Say for tax reasons that your accountant suggests that your business should be a limited partnership. As you'll recall from our earlier discussion, in every limited partnership there is at least one general partner who is personally responsible for the debts and liabilities of the limited partnership. From a control standpoint, we all want to be the general partner, but not from a liability standpoint. However, if the general partner was a corporation you controlled, you could maintain control and also enjoy the limited liability protection of a corporation.

- *Have entities own other entities*, which affords both asset protection and tax planning benefits. If not done properly, however, it can have potentially negative consequences, which is why you should consult with an attorney or accountant when implementing such a structure.

AVOID THESE PITFALLS

When using legal entities, be aware of the pitfalls to avoid when transferring assets out of your name and into the name of a legal entity. By pitfalls, I mean fraudulent transfers. Small businesspeople get themselves into trouble all the time over this one issue. If you get sued, you can't simply transfer all of your assets out of your name and into a business entity. Asset protection planning is legal and ethical when it takes place before any event occurs that may result in a claim against you. If you have already committed an act that could result in a claim, or if you have been sued, then it is too late; transfers at that time may be considered fraudulent.

There are pitfalls that can destroy the wealth you've worked so hard to build if you're not careful. Avoid mixing corporate funds and personal funds. A classic pitfall occurs when a person forms a corporation, conducts no business in the corporation, and then purchases, on the corporation's credit, personal goods such as furniture, clothing, and electronics, with the intent of never paying for these goods. The corporation's creditors will be able to "pierce the corporate veil" and file a civil suit.

Even if you keep the entity's assets separate from your own, you can lose this protection, or the protection afforded by an LLC or LP, if you fraudulently use assets. Examples include using a corporation for a type of business not allowed under the Articles of Incorporation or entering into contracts the corporation did not authorize.

Also keep in mind that we are not talking solely about civil liabilities. Criminal punishments may also result from the fraudulent use of a corporation. You are not above the law. You must follow the rules. If you're tempted, just remember that it's a lot easier to stay out of trouble than to get out of trouble.

RECORDKEEPING

Make sure you operate your business entities according to the law. First and foremost, maintain your corporate records on at least a yearly basis. When you decide to sell your company, or undergo an audit, a properly kept corporate binder can be an invaluable resource. There are two types of corporate records: initial records and annual records. Initial records include the Articles of Incorporation and various other documents that enable the officers to set up the corporate structure. Annual records include Annual Shareholder Meeting Minutes and Special Meeting Minutes.

INSURANCE: THE DEFENSE OF LAST RESORT

One question I'm often asked is whether insurance can provide enough asset protection. My answer is, "It all depends." Insurance proceeds are only paid according to the terms of the policy. With that in mind, ask yourself these two questions if you're thinking of relying on an insurance policy for asset protection:

- *What events does your policy cover?* Typically, there are only certain events covered. Damages, including punitive damages, and damages that result from an intentional act, or failure to act, won't pay you a dime.
- *What limits does my policy have?* What are your policy dollar limits, and are they enough to protect you?

Suppose an employee intentionally injures a third party, and a jury finds your business responsible for $1 million. Your policy's liability insurance has a policy limit of $50,000, and your company is only worth $200,000. It's very likely that your insurance policy doesn't cover "third-party actions." Even if it does, any judgment over $50,000 will have to come out of your business, which means you are personally liable for $750,000, because you didn't set up an alternate source of asset protection. You stand to lose both your business and your personal assets.

ESSENTIAL STEPS TO PROTECT YOUR ASSETS

Protecting your assets depends on the strength of the asset security system you design and install. Recognize this, and take these five steps to ensure that the lawsuit you face won't be the one that wipes out both your personal and business assets:

1. *Formulate a strategy.* Realize that no matter how carefully and ethically you conduct yourself and your business, it is highly likely that you may be sued.

2. *Recruit and organize professionals who can help you accomplish this goal.* Most likely, you'll need an attorney and an accountant who are both skilled at asset protection structures and methods.

3. *Prioritize your objectives.* Evaluate your overall financial situation, but in a way that doesn't negatively affect your other financial planning objectives. Consider how a transfer of assets from one entity to another may affect your tax and/or estate planning. If you put your personal residence into a limited partnership, you'll gain asset protection—but lose the tax exemption.

4. *Measure your wealth.* What assets do you have at risk, and how do you expect your wealth to change in the future?

5. *Be proactive in your planning.* You can't put an asset protection system in place after you've been sued. Unfortunately, people often think about how to protect their assets when it's too late.

One last word: A secure asset protection system in place is a lifelong process. Regular review of your assets and their vulnerabilities can ensure that you have the protection you need.

The world of asset protection is where the law and capitalism intersect, or, if you're not prepared—collide. Using all of the asset protection strategies we discussed in this chapter make good business, and legal, sense, so take advantage of them. These laws were put into place not to avoid paying deserving creditors and plaintiffs, but with one goal in mind: to encourage economic growth. Capitalism can be pretty scary at times, but a good asset security system can protect you properly; without such protection, very few people would ever try to invent something new. Be bold in your business endeavors, but also be smart by using the right tools to protect yourself.

FOR MORE INFORMATION

Visit legal publisher Nolo Press (www.nolo.com), the web site of the Internet Legal Research Group (www.ilrg.com) or my web site, www.secretmillion-aire.com. For more information about asset protection, watch for J.J.'s book, *Trump University Asset Protection 101*, to be published by John Wiley & Sons in October, 2007.

NOTES

Chapter 10: Think Like an Entrepreneur

1. Roger Fisher and William Ury, *Getting to Yes: Negotiating Agreement without Giving In* (Boston: Houghton Mifflin, 1997).
2. Charles H. Kepner and Benjamin B. Tregoe, *The Rational Manager: A Systematic Approach to Problem Solving and Decision Making* (Princeton, NJ: Kepner-Tregoe, 1997).
3. Charles H. Kepner and Benjamin B. Tregoe, *The Rational Manager: A Systematic Approach to Problem Solving and Decision Making* (Princeton, NJ: Kepner-Tregoe, 1997).
4. Alex F. Osborn, *Applied Imagination: Principles and Procedures of Creative Problem Solving*, 3rd ed. (New York: Scribner's, 1993).

Chapter 11: Start Your Own Business

1. Jeffrey A. Timmons and Stephen Spinelli, *New Venture Creation*, 7th ed. (New York: McGraw-Hill/Irwin, 2007), chap. 4.
2. Jay Conrad Levinson, *Guerrilla Marketing: Secrets for Making Big Profits from Your Small Business* (Boston: Houghton Mifflin, 1998).

Chapter 13: Why You Should Invest in Real Estate

1. In New York City and San Francisco, even older properties often sell for upwards of $800 per square foot.

2. The corresponding, inflation-adjusted, breakeven years for these dates are 1927, 1958, and 1993.
3. Most advisors recommend even less concentration. Chapter 17 more fully discusses portfolio diversification and asset allocation.

INDEX

INDEX

Habit(s): *(continued)*
  plan setting, 20, 24–27
  priority management, 20, 23–24
  spiritual health, 20, 21
  upgrading value of their time, 15
  vision, great, 20, 24, 35
  nature of, 39–40
Harvesting your business, 88
Health/stress, entrepreneurship and, 94
Helicopter-training facility, 18–19
Higher power, 22
Hill, Napoleon (*Think and Grow Rich*), 24
Hilton properties, Atlantic City, 10–11
Hinneberg family, 9
Home ownership:
  mortgage payment acceleration, 44
  national median price for single-family houses, 135, 141, 142
  refinancing or second mortgages, 68
  trap of debt in, 44, 68
Hyatt Hotel, 7–8

Idea generation, 96–99
  idea funnel, 98–99
  PEP (Proactive, Energetic, and Purposeful) approach, 98
Ideal life, visualizing your, 32–35
Identity, creating your business, 96, 105
I don't want to do a budget automatic money system. *See* Automatic money system
Income:
  investing for, 88, 128–130, 134–136, 157, 189–190
  splitting, 207
  types, and tax strategies, 203–204
    deferred, 204–205
    earned, 204
    passive, 204
    portfolio, 204
    tax-free, 205
Inertia, as obstacle to entrepreneurship, 95
Influence:
  communication as, 27

persuasion equation (five steps), 27–28
Instincts, 3, 10
Insurance:
  agents, 46, 52
  asset protection, 226
  Irrevocable Life Insurance Trust, 216
  life, 50–51, 52
  term (recommended), 51, 52
Integrity, 91
Investing/saving for retirement, 167–180
  art versus science, 170
  asset allocation (*see* Asset allocation; Portfolio management)
  Automatic Investment Plan (AIP), 50, 58–62, 64, 72, 77–78
  bonds/bond funds, 129, 140, 177–180, 188
  buying low/selling high, 17
  controlling emotions, 170
  diversification (*see* Portfolio management)
  exchange-traded funds (ETFs), 176–177
  investor comfort, five categories of, 60–62
  irrationality/rationality of markets, 170
  life stages/situations and, 190–192
  long-term focus, 170
  message of markets, versus market pundits, 170
  mutual fund selection, 175–176
  "pauper" stories, 58–59, 78
    can't afford it, 59, 78
    don't know where to put the money, 59, 78
    small amount put aside each month won't really make difference, 58–59, 78
  "playing the market," 169
  portfolio management (*see* Portfolio management)
  real estate (*see* Real estate investment)

236

90% of Americans Retire Broke.

Wealth is a Choice. What Do You Choose?

20% of the population owns 80% of the world's wealth. To belong to this 20% is your choice. You can choose to struggle to make ends meet, or you can choose to experience the freedom of living your life the way you want.

The difference between the two is… **active effort** and the **right direction.**

The Wealth Builder Action Plan gives you this right direction.

8 Programs in all, each presented by a different world-class expert.

4 Take you down four distinct pathways to wealth.

3 Establish action-orientated fundamentals that position you to win.

1 Tells you how to protect the wealth you create.

The Road to Wealth is a Choice, But Only if You Take These Steps.

Log on to www.TrumpUniversity.com/ActionPlan
or call 1-877-508-7867 to order your copy
of The Wealth Builder's Action Plan Today!

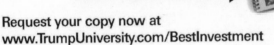

PERSONAL GOALS:

- ☑ Get promoted.
- ☑ Fire my boss.
- ☑ Start my own business.
- ☑ Buy a home.
- ☑ Flip a home.
- ☑ Enjoy financial independence.
- ☑ Live larger.
- ☑ Laugh more.
- ☑ Achieve my dreams.

START RIGHT HERE:
www.TrumpUniversity.com

Donald J. Trump knows about success. He lives it. He epitomizes it. And now he's ready to *teach* it — with world-class instructors, convenient online learning programs, and a wealth of streetwise wealth-building wisdom that can give you a lifelong professional and personal advantage.

Visit our website today — **www.TrumpUniversity.com** to learn more, do more, and BE more. The information is absolutely free — but the opportunity could be priceless.

TRUMP
UNIVERSITY

www.TrumpUniversity.com

What Do You Want Out of Life?

☐ To Just Get By

✓ To Live Your Dreams

You're about to discover **201 secrets** to achieving significant financial resources and living your life in a very BIG WAY.

Direct from Donald J. Trump and the Trump University faculty is **201 Trump Secrets of Personal Wealth**—specific personal finance strategies Donald Trump follows to grow his wealth. Best of all—these secrets are yours **FREE.**

Secrets That Will Help You:

- Cut your taxes in half
- Keep more of the money you make
- Protect your assets from lawsuits
- Reduce debt
- And more!

Get the secrets to transform your personal finances at www.TrumpUniversity.com/FinanceSecrets